PUFFIN BOOKS

Editor: Kaye Webb

THE CRIMEAN WAR

The Crimean War came after thirty-nine years of peace between the Great Powers. Though British troops were probably the best-drilled and smartest in the world – and when it came to the test they showed unbounded courage – the men at the top were not used to command. Administration broke down; the army was badly supplied with food and munitions, and the sick and wounded were neglected. For blunders, tactical errors and misunderstanding, the Crimean War has no equal in modern times. Of the 60,000 crack troops who left Britain in 1854, 43,000 were dead or disabled by January 1855. Only 7,000 of these had fallen in battle; cholera, exposure and starvation took care of the rest.

But the war did bring about enormous changes. It loosened the grip on the British Army of rich aristocrats who were soldiers because soldiering was fashionable. Public opinion, stirred up by the brilliant reports of William Russell in *The Times*, forced on the Government a radical improvement in the conditions under which men fought. And the inspired sacrifice and hard work of Florence Nightingale ensured that military hospitals at last became organized to *save* lives. The war also helped along one of the most far-reaching changes in history – the awakening of the Russian peasant from his long centuries of serfdom.

James Barbary, author of *The Boer War*, has again written a brilliant, readable and fascinating story of a war and its effects.

D1434640

JAMES BARBARY

THE CRIMEAN WAR

PUFFIN BOOKS
in association with Victor Gollancz

Penguin Books Ltd, Harmondsworth, Middlesex, England
Penguin Books Australia Ltd, Ringwood, Victoria, Australia
Penguin Books (N.Z.) Ltd, 182–190 Wairau Road, Auckland
10, New Zealand

First published by Victor Gollancz 1970
Published in Puffin Books 1975
Copyright © James Barbary, 1970

Acknowledgements

The author is obliged to Nicholas Beeching for reading his
text with a critical and expert eye. The quotes on pages 32–33
88, and 129–130, 133 are from *A Voice from the Ranks* by Timothy
Gowing, published by The Folio Society, London, for its
members in 1954.

Made and printed in Great Britain by
Cox & Wyman Ltd, London, Reading and Fakenham
Set in Intertype Baskerville

Contents

List of Illustrations

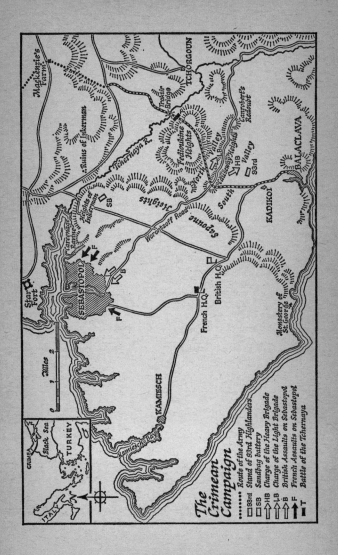

The Crimean Campaign

.... Route of the Army
☐93rd Stand of 93rd Highlanders
☐SB Sandbag battery
⇒HB Charge of the Heavy Brigade
⇑LB Charge of the Light Brigade
⇑B British Assaults on Sebastopol
⬆F French Assaults on Sebastopol
I—T Battle of the Tchernaya

MacKenzie's Farm.
Ruins of Inkerman
TCHORGOUN
Traktir Bridge
Tchernaya R.
Tedioukine Heights
North Valley
Canrobert's Redoubt
Causeway Heights
HB
93rd
BALACLAVA
South Valley
Careening Ravine
Heights of Inkerman
SB
Sapoune Heights
Woronkzoff Road
KADIKOI
Star Fort
SEBASTOPOL
F
B
F
British H.Q.
French H.Q.
Monastery of St. George
Hills
1 2
KAMIESCH
Kamiesche Bay

CRIMEA
Black Sea
TURKEY
ITALY

I

Off to War in Fancy Dress

JUNE 29th, 1854, had been an exceptionally hot day. The fading light seemed green as it came through the leafy trees surrounding Pembroke Lodge, in the midst of Richmond Park. Here, the fifteen men who governed Britain – the Cabinet – having dined together, were getting ready to transact business. Some, so the gossip ran afterwards, had dined rather too well, and stifled their yawns as they settled themselves into their leather-covered armchairs. But they tried to look attentive. There was work still to be done.

Two men, both seventy years of age, and at one time school-fellows together, at Harrow, dominated the meeting.

Lord Aberdeen, the Prime Minister, had such a reputation as a man of peace that some foreigners had begun to believe the British were unlikely any longer to act forcefully in defence of their interests. Lord Aberdeen had good personal reasons for preferring peace to war. Over forty years before, he had witnessed with his own eyes some of the horrors of Napoleon's retreat from Moscow. He had lost close friends at the Battle of Waterloo, when Napoleon had, finally, been defeated by Britain and her European allies. Lord Aberdeen privately rejoiced in the thirty-nine years of peace that had followed Waterloo. Lately with the Russians and Turks at war, Lord Aberdeen had agreed to British fleet and troop movements that might help the Turks only with extreme unwillingness. Now, with the Russian army said to be retreating across their own frontier, need any more be done?

Confronting Lord Aberdeen was a brisk, dandified man with vivid eyes. Lord Palmerston still kept about him the look of an impish schoolboy. He liked horses, and boxing, and fun. He was the most popular, experienced and hard-working man in the British Cabinet – and, some said, the most mischievous and dangerous. Lord Palmerston had long ago convinced himself that Russia could be held back from expansion into the Orient only by war. So far as he was concerned, the sooner it came the better. And the man in the street, who during thirty-nine years of peace had forgotten what the horrors of war were like, was beginning to agree with Lord Palmerston.

To the average Englishman in those days, Russia under her Tsar looked like a brutal tyranny. In the past few years the Tsar had sent in armies to crush the Poles and Hungarians when they had risen up to demand political freedom. So a war for the safety of the British Empire could, for once, be made to sound like a war for freedom. That was a debating point of which a wily politician like Lord Palmerston could take full advantage.

Palmerston watched, now, the faces of his colleagues, and noticed that none was alert. The Duke of Newcastle, the Secretary of State for War, had been droning on, reading aloud a dispatch to which not everybody was giving full attention. Even Lord Aberdeen, anxious for peace yet never sure how to achieve it, seemed to have missed the import of what, at this moment, was being read and decided. But Palmerston knew, exactly. He had hoped it might happen like this.

'*Concert measures for the siege of Sebastopol . . .*' intoned the Duke of Newcastle. Fourteen heads around him nodded what might have been approval.

Lord Palmerston was wide awake – and ready with arguments to convince those who might object; but, tonight, he had no need to argue. Such a good chance, in his opinion, might never come again. At this moment the British – like the French, under their new Emperor, Louis Napoleon, who, for reasons of his own, saw eye to eye with Palmerston about the need for war – actually had a fleet and an army, there, in

the Black Sea, within striking distance of Russia. So why not
use them?

*Her Majesty's Government will learn with regret that an
attack from which such important consequences are antici-
pated can any longer be delayed . . .'*

'Hear hear!' murmured a voice. Or might that have been
a stifled yawn?

*'Nothing but insuperable impediments should be
allowed to prevent the early decision to undertake these
operations . . .'*

The politicians nodded their assent. (Some were surprised,
afterwards, to find out how much they had agreed to.) A war
that men thought almost over was, now, about to begin.

The Russian Tsar had begun his pressure on Turkey this
time by claiming the right to protect the twelve million
Orthodox Christians living in the Turkish dominions – a
demand he knew the Sultan would never admit. Having pro-
voked the Turks into a rash declaration of war by
manoeuvres along the border, the Russian fleet had seized its
chance.

The peninsula of the Crimea, jutting southward, like a
fist, into the Black Sea, had been taken from the Turks by
Catherine the Great, in 1783. In the Crimea was a splendid
natural port – Sebastopol. The Russians had worked for the
past twenty years to build up a powerful naval base there,
and an effective war fleet.

Out of Sebastopol came the Russian fleet, under Vice-
Admiral P. S. Nakhimov. They crossed the Black Sea to the
Turkish shore, and then, with a long-range bombardment of
incendiary shells, entirely wiped out the Turkish fleet as an
effective force, as it was lying at anchor in Sinop Bay. This
left the Russians with no ship-of-war except their own afloat
on the Black Sea between the Crimea and the Turkish capital, Constantinople. Should the Russians ever reach Constantinople – and they had been trying for a hundred years –
they would be in a position to dominate the Orient.

Britain and France, both having an interest in the matter, at once moved warships near Constantinople, to protect the city and encourage the Turks. All through the spring and summer of 1854 there was desultory fighting along the Russian-Turkish frontier, the Turks on the whole getting the best of it. The Russians began to find themselves coming up against greater opposition than they had bargained for.

British and French armies, convoyed by their fleets, arrived on the Black Sea coast, to block the likeliest Russian line of advance to Constantinople. Other European powers, such as Austria, began to make sensible diplomatic overtures, in the interests of peace. The Russian armies began preparing to retreat north, across the River Pruth, which marked their own frontier – returning home to Russia.

This was the point when the fatal dispatch arrived.

The war that had seemed over was only beginning.

The dispatch sent off by the Cabinet that night had been for Lord Raglan, commander-in-chief of the British army encamped close to the Bulgarian coast, in a swampy tract, near Varna, on the shores of the Black Sea. The Russians were known to have retreated across the River Pruth. The threat to Constantinople was over. The British soldiers expected to be sent home.

Lord Raglan was a dignified, good-hearted gentleman with grey side-whiskers, and a taste for original clothes. He was sixty-six years of age. Though he began serving in the army at the age of sixteen, Lord Raglan had never so much as commanded a platoon on active service in the field, until he took up his present post. In his twenties, however, he had seen eight years of real war at first hand, having served on the Duke of Wellington's staff, during the fighting against Napoleonic armies in Portugal and Spain. He was probably the best general Britain could have called upon at that time.

Lord Raglan's personal courage was undoubted. At the famous siege of Badajoz, he had been the first into the breach, at the head of the 'forlorn hope' – the volunteer group that leads the attack. Raglan's right sleeve was pinned to the breast of his coat, empty. His cool remark to the surgeon who had amputated it, without anaesthetic, on the field of battle, was legendary. 'Here, bring that arm back. There is a ring my wife gave me, on the finger.'

He was brave, he was courteous, he was conscientious – but Lord Raglan's last thirty years had been spent at a desk, usually at the Horse Guards, the office from which the British army was then controlled. For much of that time he had been obliged to fight a paper war with politicians who, during the long years of peace, had tried to cut to the bone an army they were beginning to consider a pointless luxury.

When Lord Raglan received the dispatch to which the British Cabinet had given their yawning consent, he read it over with a grave expression, and at once sent for his senior divisional commander. Sir George Brown, of the Light Division, also aged sixty-six, was another veteran of Wellington's campaigns in the Peninsular War. Sir George, who had been Adjutant General at the Horse Guards, was a lifetime crony of Raglan's. He was a man whose candid opinion the commander-in-chief knew he could trust at this critical moment.

Sir George took the dispatch, and read it attentively. He knew that in certain London newspapers there had been irresponsible talk of invading the Crimea and attacking Sebastopol. 'The broad policy of the war,' had thundered Delane, in *The Times*, spilling ink, not blood, 'consists in striking at the heart of Russian power in the East, and that heart is Sebastopol.' But no serious and detailed plans for such an attack had been made by the army. And now the general in the field, unprepared, was being asked to turn these bold words into deeds.

'You and I are accustomed,' said Sir George Brown, 'to ask what the Duke would have done.' Sir George took the plunge. 'Without more certain information about the enemy,' he went on to say, 'the Duke would never have undertaken to invade the Crimea.'

The British had, at that moment, only the vaguest notion how many Russian troops might be waiting to meet them when they landed. Guesses varied enormously – between 40,000 and 150,000. The only maps they had were small in scale, and hopelessly out of date. Lord Raglan had not even a reliable means of knowing what the weather would be like in the Crimea at any given time of year. Would water be available? Might there be fodder for the cavalry?

All the information Lord Raglan then had about the Crimea was derived from books written some years ago by tourists who had gone there on a visit. All he knew about the defences of Sebastopol itself was derived from hasty sketches of the forts there, made by naval officers standing on deck when H.M.S. *Resolution* had entered port to deliver an ultimatum.

The Duke of Wellington, if faced with such a task, might have stood up to the politicians, and forced them by brutal common sense to change their minds. But the men now commanding the British army had grown up, all their lives, in the great Duke's shadow; they lacked his prestige; they lacked his strength of will.

'It is clear enough,' answered Lord Raglan, sadly, 'that the Government has determined on an invasion. If I do not undertake it, they will replace me by a general who will.' This was obviously true.

And what was the opinion of the Royal Navy, which would have the tricky task of landing thousands of soldiers on a hostile coast?

Admiral Dundas, commanding the British fleet in the Black Sea, gave it as his considered view that the invasion would be a death trap for the army. Yes, he could take Lord Raglan's army to the Crimea. But he could not undertake to supply it; nor, when the time came, to evacuate it.

The decision to invade had already been taken, in London and Paris. The rest was up to the fighting men.

Lord Raglan at once got in touch with his opposite number, Marshal Saint-Arnaud, commanding the French forces. Like two men ordered to leap headlong into darkness, the two generals began to coordinate their plans for an invasion of the Crimea.

Lord Raglan, for all his inexperience as a field commander, was an undoubted gentleman – a man of honour, who kept his word. The man commanding the French army, who now called himself Achilles de Saint-Arnaud, though he had been christened Jacques Arnaud Leroy, was a rogue and an adventurer – and so was his master, the new Emperor of the French.

Marshal Saint-Arnaud had done a great deal of the dirty work to help his imperial master to the throne.

Louis Napoleon, then forty-six, was the third son of the great Napoleon's younger brother. An election in 1848 had made him President of France, but four years later, by violent and illegal means, he created himself Emperor. Despite his free use of police spies, censorship, firing squads and political terror, the self-made Emperor's control of France was by no means secure.

Louis Napoleon had readily agreed with Lord Palmerston about the necessity of this war against Russia, because he wanted to dazzle the French people by glory, as his uncle had so successfully done. He daydreamed of getting revenge for the Russians' defeat of Napoleon's army in 1812. By making himself indispensable to the British, as their ally, he hoped to strengthen his position abroad. But, above all, he believed that a war might help people forget the way he had become Emperor of the French, by violently overthrowing the democratic Republic, to which, as President, he had solemnly sworn to remain faithful. Victory could make his empire popular.

And how had Leroy become Saint-Arnaud?

At sixteen, Leroy was a young soldier in the bodyguard of the French king, Louis XVIII. Peace time soldiering offered little chance of promotion. Leroy remained a second lieutenant for ten years, and won notoriety as a gambler and a debauchee, until at last an unpardonable scandal had sent him scurrying abroad, to safety.

In exile, the young officer learned English, and earned a living with his wits – travelling with a circus, marking scores in a billiard saloon, offering his services as a mercenary to the Greeks, when they fought the Turks. In 1831 he managed to procure another commission as second lieutenant, in the Foreign Legion, and went to the long-drawn-out war in Algeria, where many officers in the French army had obtained recent fighting experience.

Leroy's rapid promotion to colonel was reputedly due to his walling up five hundred Arab rebels, who had taken refuge in a cave, and asphyxiating them. A soldier with this lack of scruple was exactly the type of man for which Louis Napoleon, deep in plots to make himself Emperor, could find good use. Brought back to Paris, promoted general, and then Minister of War, Saint-Arnaud, as he now was, had been put beforehand in the right place for giving essential orders – first to the garrison of Paris, then to the firing squads – when Louis Napoleon overthrew the French Republic.

Such a man – now fifty-three, and Marshal of France – if told by his imperial master to invade the Crimea, was even less likely than Lord Raglan to voice objections. Lean, wiry, glibly charming, Saint-Arnaud, as he gave the necessary orders, knew in his heart, however, that he was close to the end of his career of double-dealing. The billiard marker, the circus performer, the cheat, might now command a French army, in a uniform that glittered magnificently with gold braid. But he was a dying man. Saint-Arnaud, as he talked over with Lord Raglan the problems of the invasion, knew that the angina painfully racking his breast would soon kill him, yet still he clung to command.

On 14 February 1854, amid ringing cheers from the crowded pavements, the six-footers of the first battalion of the Coldstream Guards had gone marching through grey London from their quarters in St George's Barracks. At

Waterloo Station a troop train waited, to take them on the first stage of their long journey east, to help hold off the Russians from Constantinople.

The men marched incomparably well – arms and legs swinging with precision. Not only had even the oldest of them marching through the streets experienced far more parade-ground drill than actual fighting, their uniforms were more like fancy dress than combat wear. For years now, regimental officers, who, in the Guards, wore blue frock coats, had vied with each other to produce uniforms, as well as men, that would look impressive at ceremonial drill. The Coldsteams' scarlet jackets were trimmed with gold. Their bright blue trousers were extremely tight. Huge black bearskin caps exaggerated the men's height, and the white belts crossing on the scarlet jackets made them look abnormally broad-chested. Gleaming brass buckles shone in the winter sun.

Each man's pack weighed thirty pounds, each rifle more than ten pounds – a not excessive weight. Yet, when the tall soldiers, behind the brisk drumbeats of their line of little drummer boys, finally reached the troop train, they felt they had marched three times the distance. They were choked by the stiff leather stock which each Guardsman wore under his chin to force his head erect. Marching with a pack in a stock was slow torture.

In the train, the huge bearskin caps bumped ridiculously against the railway roofs. Though the winter morning was cold, they had no greatcoats. Little did they know it, but the Coldstream Guards would soon be sent off to war with no tents for the rank-and-file, no proper stores, no transport, and hardly any medical supplies.

'*The scum of the earth, enlisted for drink.*' The Iron Duke's description of the men who won him the battle of Waterloo was perhaps harsh and condescending, but there was truth in it. Not many men joined the ranks of the British army in those days, unless they were forced to. The three most common reasons for enlistment were unemployment, drink, or being jilted by a sweetheart.

Once he put on uniform, however, and accepted discipline, the British soldier was renowned for his displays of exceptional courage. His favourite weapon was the bayonet. Indeed, as the army was then organized, the private soldier got little chance to practise firing. Musketry practice rarely occurred, and usually took the form of an unofficial 'firelock competition', when officers would lay bets on the marksmanship of the men from their respective regiments. The soldiers were expected to fire at a target a hundred yards off, usually a crude outline of a French grenadier. If they managed to hit any part of him, they had done well.

But although sheer valour in this campaign would count much, marksmanship was also becoming important. A scientific change was coming over warfare. Trafalgar had been fought by sailing ships at the mercy of wind and weather, and by soldiers firing flintlock muskets with an effective range of only a hundred yards. But by 1854, though the ships of the Royal Navy might still carry a full set of sails, they also had auxiliary engines. Ships of the line were driven by propellers, and there were paddle steamers to work close inshore. Moreover the rifle, recently improved in France, was about to dominate the battlefield.

The French, grenadiers and all, were now Britain's ally (though Lord Raglan, mentally living in the past, would sometimes absentmindedly refer to the common enemy as 'the French' instead of 'the Russians'). Many units of the British army were being armed with adaptations of a French secret weapon, on which, since the year 1847, Captain Minié of the Chasseurs d'Orléans had been working. This invention – a reliable muzzle-loading rifle – was to give the British and French their one initial advantage over the armies of the Tsar in the Crimea.

A rifled barrel imparts a spin to a bullet, so that it goes a longer distance in a straighter trajectory. Captain Minié's new rifle was sighted up to a thousand yards. For the first three hundred yards, it would fire dead straight, and it penetrated much further than a musket bullet.

The loose-fitting ball of a musket dropped easily down the smooth barrel, and a touch of the ramrod would nudge it home. With the old-fashioned muzzle-loading rifle, the ball had sometimes to be forced down the rifling by tapping it with a mallet – not a safe or quick procedure amid the roar of battle.

Into the base of a loose-fitting lead bullet, like a musket ball, Minié had inserted a small iron cup. The ball would drop easily down the barrel, but the charge, when exploding, drove the iron cup into the soft lead at the bullet's base. The cup flared out, to grip the rifling, and spin the bullet straight and true.

The British soldiers in camp at Varna near the Black Sea coast could count on the new muzzle-loading rifle, and their own natural courage. But almost everything else that might be necessary in an invasion had been neglected, forgotten, ignored or left behind.

As the Coldstream Guards marched down to the wooden jetties that had been run out from the beach at Balchick Bay, near Varna, – there to hang around killing time during an ill-organized embarkation that lasted ten days – the difference in their appearance was extraordinary. The Guards were all growing beards.

The rigid and painful leather stock, useful for keeping the soldier's head impressively erect on parade, had now been cast aside. Permission had been given to grow beards. The shako – a piece of impractical headgear more suitable for comic opera than active service – was to be replaced by the forage cap. All this was a gain.

But the Guardsmen, those giants of men who had marched with a swing through the streets of London carrying forty pounds of equipment, were now putting forth all their strength to cover the few miles to the jetty in Balchick Bay, while their knapsacks were loaded on packhorses that trailed behind.

From Marseilles, the French had brought with them to the Black Sea an enemy more dangerous and deadly even than the Russians: cholera. It played a bigger role in the Crimean War than any weapon or feat of generalship: it was the enemy that neither side had come prepared to fight.

Asiatic cholera attacks between one and five days after the comma-shaped bacteria have entered the human body by means of contaminated water or food. The victim suffers a purging diarrhoea, vomiting, hiccoughing, and agonizing cramps in his leg muscles. Half those who catch cholera can expect to die, if the disease is not treated – but skilled nursing, even in the days before modern medicine, could reduce this terrible death-rate to one in ten. Cholera can best be kept in check by strict control of sanitation and water supply. The effective answer to cholera is cleanliness.

Soldiers of both the French and British armies took the comma-shaped bacteria with them, inside their bodies, into the fleet of transports waiting offshore, in Balchick Bay. Since medical science then held that cholera was spread by germs blown on the wind, not only were sick men ordered to stay below decks, in airless conditions that kept getting filthier and filthier, but tens of thousands of fit men were kept below decks, too, until they also began to succumb to the disease.

In two out of the four days that the vast convoy of ships took to sail to the Crimea, H.M.S. *Britannia* alone recorded 109 deaths – and this was before any soldier aboard had yet heard a shot fired in anger. It was now September of 1854.

2

The Capture of the Great Redoubt

As the six hundred vessels of the vast British-French allied convoy crawled along at three knots towards the low brown cliffs of the Crimean coast, the Russians were given their chance to end the conflict before it had even begun. Each allied steamer towed two sailing ships; each line of ships was led by a man-of-war; and those long rows of slow-moving ships were vulnerable to gunfire.

In Sebastopol – the five-mile-long, mile-wide, land-locked harbour cut into the west coast of the Crimea by the mouth of the river Tchernaya – a powerful Russian war fleet rode at anchor. There were fifteen line-of-battle ships, as well as some frigates and brigs, a large war steamer, the *Vladimir*, and eleven smaller steamers. Had they been brought out boldly to attack the Allied flotilla as the men were trying to disembark, the Russian ships of war might well have wrecked all chances of an organized landing.

Vice Admiral Nakhimov had revelled, not long since, in the destruction of a weaker Turkish fleet at anchor in the port of Sinop. Helplessly outranged, the Turkish ships had been sitting ducks for Russian incendiary shells. But neither Nakhimov nor his commander, Admiral Kornilov, relished facing the broadsides of British and French men-of-war. As the vast fleet of transports slowly approached the Crimea, the Russian admirals kept their warships safe under the fortress guns of Sebastopol harbour.

Meanwhile, Lord Raglan cruised nonchalantly up and down the coast, trying to decide where to land.

South of Sebastopol, the navy took him to a small deep-water inlet near a village of five hundred inhabitants, called

Balaclava. Here Lord Raglan's ship lingered offshore, observing the pretty wooden houses surrounded by their vineyards and gardens, examining the ruined Genoese fort on the headland. He decided, however, to cruise farther north, and look there for a stretch of coast where his 26,000 infantry, 1,000 cavalry and 60 guns could be landed more quickly than in the confined anchorage of Balaclava.

Sailing north, Lord Raglan passed very close to the fortress city of Sebastopol. Along the south bank of the estuary anchorage he could see the Russian Black Sea Fleet swinging at anchor. He observed the vast arsenal, the dockyard, the dome of the half-finished church. On the harbour's north bank, the great octagonal Star Fort covered the city's landward approaches.

Yet still farther northward Raglan steamed, gazing ashore on low cliffs intersected by rivers – the Balbek, the Katcha, and the Alma. Boats could easily enough be beached on the gently sloping shores of a river mouth. But if the Russians were to mount guns on those dominating cliffs to left and right, they could create a shambles.

At last, thirty-five miles to the north of his objective, Lord Raglan encountered what he had been hoping to find – and what a more efficient military intelligence might have discovered for him long before – a broad shingle beach, protected inland from cavalry attacked by a shallow lagoon. The allied armies could land there safely under cover of the ships' heavy guns, which would outrage any field guns the Russian artillery might bring to attack their flanks.

The moment of landing was the riskiest of all. Surely this was the time the Russians would attack? But so far there was not a sign of them, either on land or sea.

The navy landed the British army in brisk and masterly fashion, the bluejackets sometimes carrying the soldiers bodily ashore when they were too sick to walk through the surf. When the British and French armies set foot in Calamita Bay, the cholera of course came with them.

Much that was essential to the army's well-being and

effectiveness had, however, been left behind in the chaos of departure. Six thousand pack animals had been abandoned in Bulgaria, so the British army landed with no transport whatever. The French were better off where transport was concerned, and even had ambulances, an amenity so far unheard of among the British. The French, though, had no cavalry – and only a thousand British light horsemen got ashore to act as the eyes of the army. The Heavy Brigade, less quick across country, but more effective in a charge during battle, were to be landed later. In a campaign such as this, over unknown country, where the available maps were bad, cavalry would be indispensable to the army – a force to be kept intact, and not risked in any wild skirmishes or heroic battle charges. ('I kept my cavalry in a bandbox,' said Lord Raglan afterwards.)

The French, once ashore, set up bivouac. Each French soldier carried in his pack one third of a small tent that he shared with two comrades. After a day of bright sunshine, that night it started to rain; in the Crimea, the weather could change with disconcerting suddenness. The French rank and file spent the night under canvas, while the British were soaked to the skin, because tents had been landed only for the officers.

But the soldiers had a reason to be glad for the rain. The British army had been landed desperately short of water, and then given salt rations. The inland lagoon was brackish. As boots and hooves churned up the ground to filthy mud, the thirsty British soldiers began, that night, to quench their thirst from muddy pools.

Cholera, a waterborne disease, can strike quickly. Within the first forty-eight hours after the landing, one thousand British soldiers were rowed back to the sick transports in the fleet moored offshore.

So far, the Russians had made no appearance, despite the chances given them by Lord Raglan's leisurely preparations for landing. After a lapse of time, one Cossack officer in a bottle-green uniform with silver lace, escorted by some

shabby-looking Cossack lancers, rode to the crest of a distant
hill, out of gunshot, and calmly took notes.

A detachment of light cavalry, under Lord Cardigan,
went off to scour the countryside, and came back with a
useful haul – three hundred arabas, or wooden country carts,
each with a carrying capacity of more than half a ton. Their
Tartar drivers were enrolled for wages. The British army
luckily now had transport, but those Tartar drivers would all
be dead by the end of the first winter campaign.

Despite chaos and cholera, the drenching rain overnight,
and the thirst brought on by their cold rations of salt pork
and ship's biscuit, the British army in the bright sun of next
morning made as brave and gay a muster as the better-
equipped French.

In blue jackets and bright red trousers, wearing their
distinctive peaked caps with narrow crowns, the French
marched nearest to the sea. They were to advance under
cover of the guns of the allied fleet, which proceeded
offshore, landing supplies, taking off the sick, keeping a
watchfully protective eye over the marching men. The
French made their way south, towards Sebastopol, in a diamond formation. At the rear of the diamond were men in
more picturesque and varied uniforms still – a force of Turks,
ill-found conscripts whose fine soldierly qualities the allies
were only slowly and grudgingly to accept as the campaign
proceeded.

The British, as if still on parade in Hyde Park, marched
their men in two double columns, with bands playing and
flags flying. Their uniforms were spectacular. Conspicuous
among them were the Highlanders – kilted giants with bare
knees, each man carrying the traditional broadsword.

Uniforms of the other regiments of the line were a be-
wilderment of scarlet slashed with white crossed belts, and
green, and royal blue. They marched across the crisp, sweet-
smelling turf of the Crimean downland with parade-ground
precision – only broken as the leading ranks approached the
river Bulganak, when, for a moment, discipline of the des-

perately thirsty men broke, and all but the Highlanders ran
to stoop at the stream and fill their water bottles.

If the British infantry were spectacular to watch, the thousand cavalrymen protecting the allied armies' inland flank
were so gaudy as to be almost theatrical. The Hussars, like
the Horse Artillery, wore furred pelisses laced with gold.
Many cavalry regiments wore plumes. The cavalry was the
fashionable branch of the British army, and wealthy commanders of crack regiments poured small fortunes into
making dandies of their men. Those uniformed horsemen
advanced, however, with a precision that contradicted
their almost effeminate gaudiness. So far as drill and courage
went, they were, in fact, the best light cavalry in Europe.

What of the Russians – the enemy over the hill?

Russia in 1854 was a rigid despotism. All power lay in the
hands of the Tsar, who governed through an army, a civil
service, and a church over which he had almost complete
personal authority. Russia was then an agricultural country
where the best land was owned by nobles and country
gentry. This land was worked for these masters by millions
of serfs. Russian serfs were tied to the land. If a master
granted a serf permission to open a store, the master had to
be paid a share of the profits. When the land was sold, the
serfs were sold along with it, like cattle.

The Russian conscripts, in their grey army coats that
reached down to the ankle, were mostly armed with out-
dated, brass-bound, muzzle-loading muskets. Though brave
and naturally talented, they tended to give dumb and servile
obedience to their officers. They were men scarcely even beginning to dream of those ordinary political freedoms that
the English, French, and Americans had long held to be the
inalienable rights of man.

A few years earlier, in 1849, a Russian army, like the one
now defending the Crimea, had entered Hungary, and brut-
ally crushed a rising for freedom. In civilized Europe, just
then, the Russians were not loved. This though was hardly a

good reason for the troops of civilized European nations to invade soil that had been Russian at least since 'Crim Tartary' was taken into the Russian Empire, after an earlier war with the Turks, seventy years before.

Under a despotic government, much depends on the personality of the autocrat. Nicholas was fifty-eight years old, and had been Tsar since 1825. He was by upbringing a soldier.

Personally, Nicholas had no liking for serfdom. But any impulse he may have felt, early in his reign, towards mild reform was soon checked by his fear that even small changes in the order of society might bring closer a revolution. He decided to militarize Russia. The Tsar put not only state officials but students and even shopkeepers into specially designed compulsory uniforms. He organized the Russian political police – the innocuously named Third Section of the Private Chancery of the Emperor, which spied not only on political actions but also on dangerous ideas. He imposed a strict censorship – blue-pencilling the work of the great Russian poet Pushkin with his own hand, because he could not trust others to be severe enough. He was named the Iron Tsar. The serfs in the countryside had another name for him. During the early years of his reign, they had often risen up against the oppression of their masters, only to be shot and flogged into submissiveness. They nicknamed their Tsar *Nicholas Palkin* – Nicholas the Flogger.

But the Iron Tsar had a childish side, too. One room in his palace was filled with toy soldiers; he would sneak off and play with them. He was in fact treating Russia – economically and politically backward, though it was the largest country in Europe – like yet another big roomful of toy soldiers.

The Tsar's commanding general in the Crimea, Prince Menshikov, was now nearly seventy. Like most of the British generals he was up against, Prince Menshikov had seen service in the Napoleonic Wars. A tactless, unintelligent man he had been the Tsar's Ambassador to Constantinople in the year before war broke out. His heavy-handedness there had done much to increase the chances of war. He was deeply mistrusted by the younger and more capable officers, many of them eager patriots, who served obediently in the Russian army now slowly mobilizing in the hills to confront the allies on their march south to Sebastopol.

The hostile armies met where the River Alma cut its meandering way through the pleasant, turf-covered plateau across which the allies had been marching, and flowed down between cliffs to the sea. On the facing hillside, Russian guns commanded the long grassy slope of the Alma's far bank, beyond which a large Russian army had been mustered – 40,000 men and 200 guns. Here, on the heights of Alma, General Menshikov had decided to make a defensive stand.

His own guns dominated the approaches to the river, chiefly from an earthwork called by the British 'The Great Redoubt'. He had taken up a position, General Menshikov told subordinates, that could never be carried by direct assault.

Suppose the British and French advanced within range of his guns and tried to wade the Alma. The red clay bank was in places fifteen feet high – a natural escarpment. Above it, the allied soldiers must march upward – under hostile cannon fire and musketry fusillade – slowly and breathlessly up a long, steep, grassy slope, devoid of cover.

Should the feeble British cavalry force of only 1,000 sabres attempt any outflanking movement inland, they would soon find themselves confronted by Russian cavalry out-numbering them nearly five to one. The allies, in Prince Menshikov's opinion, could neither turn his position, nor assault it. So confident was he of victory that the Prince brought out with him from Sebastopol a picnic party of thirty young ladies, to watch the thrilling sight of a Russian victory.

They were in raptures at their distant glimpse of scarlet British uniforms.

The chief difficulty for the French, who were nearest the sea, would be to get at grips with the enemy. Their attack must begin by scaling the cliffs that came down to the shore. However, since Prince Menshikov considered those cliffs unassailable, he had stationed no troops at the top, so, even when the French had gallantly scrambled up, they were still a long way from the fighting.

This, anyway, was Marshal Saint-Arnaud's last chance for glory. As the French commander rode across the lines to confer with Lord Raglan, the British noted his rigid posture, his hollow, pain-racked features. Saint-Arnaud, though personally a brave man, was in fact no army commander. To serve as his plan of attack, he pencilled some arrows boldly across his small-scale map, in the general direction of the foe. On the morning of the battle, Marshal Saint-Arnaud spoke with grandiloquent magnificence to his divisional generals: *'With such men as you, I have no orders to give! I have but to point to the enemy.'* Tactically, that certainly simplified matters.

For years now, professional soldiers had argued the relative merits of advancing in column against advancing in line. During the Battle of Alma, at the beginning of the epoch of rifle fire, this tactical dispute was to be effectively tested in action.

Until that time, troops armed with muskets had been obliged to march to within a hundred yards of the enemy, and fire off rapid volleys at close range. Therefore, in those days, parade-ground drills were not merely ceremonial, but a disciplined form of combat training, since to deliver their volleys of musketry on the field of battle with maximum effect, the troops must march and wheel and deploy, yet always keep their ranks dressed precisely, as when on the parade ground.

If infantrymen went into action massed in columns, many

men deep, the braver soldiers would reassure the more timid, and, at the moment when the foe arrived close enough, the weight of the column's massed volley would be devastating. Such a solid column of men, though, was vulnerable to artillery. The cannonball from one enemy gun, taking a column in the flank, could tear a hole through the ranks of living flesh from end to end. Even the conical bullet from a Minié rifle, since its penetrative power was much greater than that of a musket ball, would kill two or three men at once when fired into a column.

A general like Prince Menshikov, in charge of a conscript army, could never be confident of the quality and discipline of the men under his command. But he knew that conscript reinforcements would soon arrive, to replace the men he might lose. Such generals were firmly in favour of manoeuvring in column.

The British army, by contrast, though small, was highly disciplined, and the men served as soldiers for a lifetime. An infantryman drilled to the pitch of perfection exemplified by the Guards and the Highlanders could not quickly be replaced; but the excellence of their drill, and their natural aggressiveness, made it technically possible for such British troops to be deployed on the battlefield not in column, but in a line only two men deep.

They were capable of marching in this frail formation under a hail of hostile fire – an endless line of riflemen that could scarcely be outflanked, and through which no gunfire could tear paralysingly large holes. As individual soldiers fell, those still on their feet would automatically, unthinkingly, close up and dress the line. Such a battlefield manoeuvre, however, depended on almost superhuman discipline – a self-control in the troops enabling them to march through shot and shell much as if they were on parade – until they came to the yelling crescendo of their bloody onset.

The Battle of Alma, on 20 September 1854 was, by and large, fought line against column. Lord Raglan was able to exercise little control over the course of the battle. He first rode up and down the British advanced line, slowly, on his bay charger Shadrach, in his plumed cocked hat, a conspicuous target for enemy sharpshooters, giving his men a reassuring display of cold courage. He then took up a position on a knoll a long way forward, with his staff clustered around him.

Lord Raglan's post of observation was, in fact, so far forward as almost to be inside enemy lines – and so far off that orders he gave did not often arrive in time to be of effect. But his men were encouraged, as they advanced, to see him there, in a place of danger.

The first British infantry to extend in a long scarlet line, cross that river, and march up the shot-torn turf of the naked hillside to the very muzzles of the Russian guns massed in the Great Redoubt were the Royal Fusiliers.

Timothy Gowing, a Baptist minister's son, then twenty years of age, had volunteered for service in the Crimea, where he fought in the ranks of the Fusiliers. In an account that he pieced together long after, he gives us an idea of what a young soldier felt on that day at Alma as he crossed the river and made the long climb up the hill:

Away we went at a steady pace, until about midday. Presently, they began to pitch their shot and shell among us, and our men began to fall. I know that I felt horribly sick – a cold shivering running through my veins, but I am happy to say the feeling passed off, as soon as I began to get warm to it. It was very exciting work, and the sights were sickening.

We had deployed into line, and were presently ordered to lie down, to avoid that hurricane of shot and shell. The enemy had the range to a nicety.

We still kept advancing, and then lying down again. Our men's feelings were now wrought up to such a state that it was not an easy matter to stop them. Up to the river we rushed, and got ready for a swim. A number of our poor fellows were drowned, or shot down with grape and canister. Into the river we dashed, nearly up to our armpits, with our ammunition and rifles on the top of our heads to keep them dry, scrambled out the best way we could, and commenced to ascend the hill.

We were only about 600 yards from the mouths of the guns; the thunderbolts of war were, therefore, not far apart – and death loves a crowd. The havoc among the Fusiliers was awful. There were 14 guns of heavy calibre just in front of us, and others on our flanks – in all, some 42 guns were raining death and destruction on us.

Up the hill we went, step by step. The fighting now became very exciting, we firing and advancing all the time. My comrade said to me, 'We shall have to shift those fellows with the bayonet, old boy,' pointing to the Russians.

Our noble Colonel Yea, and in fact all our mounted officers, were encouraging us to move on. General Codrington waved his hat, then rode straight at one of the embrasures, and leaped his grey Arab into the breast of the work. Others, breathless, were soon beside him.

With a ringing cheer we topped the heights, and into the enemy's battery we jumped, spiked the guns, and bayoneted or shot down the gunners.

Since Prince Menshikov had from the start taken up a defensive position, the Great Redoubt with all its commanding guns was the key to the battlefield.

Against the two thousand British infantry now inside the vital earthwork, the Russian High Command detached four battalions of the Vladimir Regiment. Three thousand men wearing long grey coats advanced on the Redoubt in heavy columns. The Fusiliers had aimed their rifles when some unknown voice shouted, 'For God's sake, don't fire! Here come the French!'

The mistake – that moment of agonized hesitation – was decisive. In a few moments, the Russian mass was pouring down upon them, and had thrust them out. All the men of Codrington's Brigade who so far had reached the Great Redoubt began to be driven downhill.

But up the hill towards the Russian guns now came marching the Guards. 'Ceremoniously, and with dignity', the Coldstream and Grenadier Guards were advancing through smoke and shot as calmly as if they were engaged in a parade-ground evolution. At their side were the High-landers, under Sir Colin Campbell. When six massive Russian columns turned their fire on the advancing British line, the Highlanders charged with raised broadsword.

By now the French artillery were in the fray. As the kilted Highlanders came forward at the charge, the fire of the French field guns took the Russian columns in the left flank. As cannonballs tore their lines from end to end, the Russians broke formation and gave ground. With a cheer the Guards marched into the Great Redoubt, from which they were not to be shifted.

Now that this key artillery position had been wrested from him and the British right wing had doggedly pushed its way to the heights of Alma on the seaward of the Redoubt, Prince Menshikov's army was in danger of being trapped between the British and the cliffs along the shoreline. The Russians had no choice but to withdraw their army helter-skelter, using their numerous cavalry to cover their flight.

'If we only had three or four thousand cavalry with us,' commented Timothy Gowing, 'they would not have got off quite so cheaply.'

The British had lost 1,893 men killed and wounded, and the Russians 5,500. The high-velocity Minié bullets had done their deadly work on the dense Russian columns. Lord Raglan estimated that the French, who came late into the engagement, probably lost about 560 men.

When Raglan urged an energetic pursuit of the defeated foe, Marshal Saint-Arnaud insisted, with depressing punctilio, that the French infantry must first, of course, return to the place where, that morning, they had taken off their knapsacks, and put them on again. The dispatch to the Emperor in Paris would resonate with glory, but the chance of keeping the Russians on the run was to be lost.

The allies waited two days on the battlefield, burying all the dead in huge pits. The British wounded, and those who continued to sicken from cholera, were carried bodily by their comrades down to the ships, and transported thence across the Black Sea, to two British army hospitals that had been set up at Scutari, on the shores of the Bosphorus facing Constantinople.

3

The Thin Red Line

The Times was in 1854 probably the most influential news-paper in the world – truculent, lively, committed to reform. Under Delane, its brilliant editor, it reflected the opinion of the solid British middle class with an authority that gave it the nickname 'The Thunderer'. More than once, during the Crimean War, the fulminations of *The Times* made the British government itself tremble. But, on occasion, even *The Times* could be horribly wrong.

The subconscious or accidental lies of a popular news-paper are usually what its readers want or expect to hear. After the Battle of Alma. *The Times* ran a headline: *The Fall of Sebastopol: Decisive Intelligence,* and went on to report.

It may now be confidently stated that the forts of Sebastopol fell successively before the combined forces of the assailants . . . on 26th at latest, Prince Menshikov surrendered the place. The battles are over, and the victory is won.

But the famous newspaper was merely saying – on totally wrong information – what everyone in Britain expected to hear. With the Russian field army defeated at Alma and in full and bewildered retreat, what on earth was there to stop the allies marching at once upon Sebastopol, and taking the city by storm before autumn turned to winter?

Lord Raglan may have lacked the vigorously enterprising qualities of a born field commander, but he was no fool; he had common sense. He knew as well as the next man that the more rapidly the allied armies could be pushed on to Sebastopol, the better were their chances of finding the city defenceless.

Marshal Saint-Arnaud's mind, however, no longer had a grip on the urgencies of this war. When, after Alma, the allied generals and their staff conferred on the next move, the French Marshal sat rigidly upright in his chair, hardly speaking. But unless, as French commander-in-chief, he gave his full support, a dash for Sebastopol was out of the question. 'Did you observe Saint-Arnaud?' said Lord Raglan to a friend after the conference. 'He is dying.' Within a week he was dead.

This delay after Alma gave the Russians a miraculously unexpected second chance.

François Canrobert, a forty-five-year-old divisional general who had seen service in Algeria, took over command of the French army from Marshal Saint-Arnaud. Canrobert was physically brave yet morally timid. Supreme command unnerved him. He had already begun to be disheartened by French losses from cholera.

Canrobert knew that his meteoric rise in the French army was due not so much to his own military distinction as to the way he had served his master, Louis Napoleon, in the conspiracy against the French Republic two years before. In Paris, the firing squads that had shot down in cold blood tens of thousands of Frenchmen for the crime of being loyal republicans had been commanded by a man called Canrobert. The fact was known, and unforgotten.

The French might be unlucky in the choice of their new commander, but the Russians had stumbled on a man who was equal to the crises of the time. Thirty-six years old, he was an engineer officer of German origin from Russia's Baltic Provinces. In mind and manner, Col. E. I. Todleben was a striking contrast to the dashing aristocrats who usually officered the Russian army. The Colonel was studious, enormously competent, diabolically energetic, and brave in a quiet and unspectacular way.

Colonel Todleben had been ordered to go to Sebastopol in good time, and patch up the fortifications there. Prince Menshikov protested that he simply wasn't wanted. The allies would never be so foolish as to invade the Crimea. (A few days later, they landed.) Prince Menshikov had actually applied to the Tsar to have this boring and pestiferous German engineer officer sent back to St Petersburg, when the defeat at Alma gave him something else to think about.

Unwanted, rebuffed, ignored, Colonel Todleben quickly continued to work on his plans for improving the fortification of Sebastopol, even though the commanding general had curtly informed him that his plans were too grandiose – and anyway, would cost far too much money.

Given time to fortify – and time was now the key to everything – Colonel Todleben was privately confident that Sebastopol could be defended for many months to come. Fortified, the chances in favour of the city's holding out in a long siege were far better than could ever have seemed possible to allied optimists, such as the man who sent that false news to the London *Times*.

Though Sebastopol's army garrison now numbered only three thousand – Menshikov having marched most of his men inland to maintain a line of communication with Russia – thousands of sailors, all trained gunners, could be landed from the fleet.

Only the key fort defending the great naval base from the south, a 28-foot high semicircular redoubt called Malakoff, was built of stone. The city's ring of wall was defended, otherwise, by earthen batteries that might look impressive from a distance, but which had been dug years before, and now were crumbling.

However, the uniformed peasants of Russia's conscript army knew better than most how to handle pick and shovel. Given a modest allowance of time and a leader who knew what he was doing, the forts around the city could be effectively strengthened, and armed with new batteries of naval guns. The worst risk, for the Russians, was that the powerful allied fleet offshore might steam into Sebastopol harbour and from close range bombard and destroy the city. So why not block the harbour entrance?

Here Colonel Todleben found an ally more to his liking than pompous Prince Menshikov. Admiral Kornilov was perhaps not a great seagoing admiral, but he was a bluff sailor and a stout-hearted Russian patriot. Admiral Kornilov, at Todleben's suggestion, after removing the guns from seven of his warships, had them scuttled in a line across the harbour mouth. From then on, the Russians, systematically, began to dig in. By 26 September, the fortress was armed with 172 pieces of ordnance, many of them heavy naval guns.

At last, the allies began their dilatory march towards Sebastopol. To their amazement, the enemy they believed defeated had thrown up a new gun emplacement beyond the Balbek River, threatening their left flank. Beyond, Lord Raglan could see the great Star Fort, dominating Sebastopol harbour's northern shore – a forty-year-old earth fort, with walls ten feet thick, protected by an eighteen-foot ditch and mounting 47 guns. At Star Fort was the fresh-turned earth of more new batteries yet, dug threateningly to left and right. Beyond, in the harbour, the broadsides of the Russian naval vessels still afloat had been aimed directly at the oncoming allied armies.

From the distance, Star Fort looked like a powerful obstacle, though Colonel Todleben himself later admitted that, in fact, at that moment, there was almost nothing to stop the allies from walking straight into Sebastopol. What held back the British and French that fine autumn morning was not the reality of the Russian threat, but their own hesitation. They were moving slowly and blindly.

The Russians had posted a lookout by the top window of the Naval Library inside Sebastopol – a high vantage point from which the country for miles around could be observed. On 25 September he saw a flash of scarlet uniforms on the march through scrub woodland to the north of Sebastopol harbour. Scarlet indicated the British. But, to the lookout's surprise, the British infantry appeared to be leading its own cavalry – an incredible way to march on active service.

Not liking the look of Star Fort, the allies had evidently decided to make a wide detour around Sebastopol, and to attack the city's southern fortifications.

When the news was told to him, Colonel Todleben answered with one of his rare smiles. What Sebastopol needed most desperately was time. Todleben already had full plans for making the city's southern approaches impregnable – but his men needed time to dig, and this the enemy were now giving him.

Lord Raglan knew the risks of the flank march, but they had been forced upon him, and he accepted them. His men would have to part company with the protective guns of the British fleet. They would be marching across unknown terrain, sandwiched between the garrison of Sebastopol and a large Russian field army operating somewhere inland. Success would depend on his cavalry brigade – the thousand gaudily dressed light horse.

Since a mounted man can cover country at three or four times the pace of a man on foot, the cavalry serves as the eyes and ears of an army on the move. Its job now would be to get out well ahead and cover each flank – to probe for the whereabouts of the enemy, yet mask from Russian sight Lord Raglan's own intentions.

This was exactly the moment Lord Lucan, commanding the British cavalry, chose to get lost.

At half past eight that morning, Lord Lucan had led his troopers down a track through scrub woodland, ahead of the infantry. He might have been riding out, lightheartedly, to a fox hunt. He sent no scouts out ahead to find a way for his main force.

When he came to a fork in the road, he guessed, reasonably enough, as he would on a day's hunting, that the larger of the two paths would lead where he needed to go. But the larger path petered out amid brushwood and scrub oak. From that moment on, Lucan was obliged to push his thousand horsemen south-east blindly, in disorganized fashion, across rough country, on a compass bearing that hopefully might bring him out of the wood.

Meanwhile, Lord Raglan's infantry, too, had lost formation. They had to work their way southward through brushwood, like beaters through a covert. Lord Raglan and his mounted staff, having waited to see the foot soldiers well on their way, then cantered along the road down which Lord Lucan's cavalry had gone. Luckily, at the fork, the General knew the way.

Lord Raglan was, by now, a long way ahead of his army. Airey, his Quartermaster General, generally acted as Lord Raglan's chief of staff. Galloping ahead, General Airey came to the place where the woodland track rejoined the main road – and ran headlong into the rearguard of the army Prince Menshikov was sending inland. There rumbled the Russian wagon train, protected by thick ranks of infantry.

This was a moment when the wildest bluff might work.

Seeing the white plumes and the bloodstock horses of high-ranking British officers emerge from the woodland, the Russian rearguard commander took fright. Those were the victors of Alma. Surely, the entire British army must lie nearby, hidden in ambush.

Lord Raglan got the point quickly. He reined in, and looked as dignified and confident as he knew how – as if the Russian rearguard were impertinent intruders. The Russian commander stared back, amazed.

The British horse artillery clattered up soon after, and a few shots from their guns broke the spell. Russians by the thousand ran away as fast as they could. The bluff had succeeded.

Lucan, having imperilled the whole army, finally broke cover with his struggling cavalry. Lord Raglan's anger, this once, almost showed through his habitual courtesy. Frigidly he said, 'Lord Lucan – you are late!' A mild rebuke for such incompetence, but, in Lord Lucan's mind, those words continued to rankle bitterly. With Lord Lucan, every breath of criticism rankled.

*

Lord Wolseley, who was to attain the rank of Commander-in-Chief of the British army, wrote years later of officers such as Lucan, whom, as a junior, he had watched exercising command in the Crimea: *Had they been private soldiers, I don't think any colonel would have made them corporals.*

The cavalry was that branch of the army which, through forty prosperous years of peace, had attracted men of wealth and fashion. Cavalry officers with their sweeping side whiskers were London's lady killers. They had developed a remarkable style of dressing and talking. They spoke in languid voices, and made a careful point of never pronouncing the letter R (something unpleasant would be spoken of by a British cavalry officer at the time as *vewwy howwid*).

Their tiny waists were tightly corseted, they continually smoked big cigars, but they rode like the very devil. They had almost no aptitude normally sought in a leader of men during war except blind personal courage. As an experienced French cavalry commander once remarked, 'The British cavalry officer seems to be impressed by the conviction that he can dash or ride over everything, as if the art of war were precisely the same as that of fox hunting.'

An officer's commission was his property, which he could buy or sell. To enable a rich young man in a fashionable regiment to rise a step in rank, vast sums would change hands. Lord Lucan himself, for example, when a young blood of twenty-six, had paid £25,000 of the time to become lieutenant colonel of the 17th Lancers, when the regular purchase price was £5,000.

The regiment's senior major was then Anthony Bacon, a Peninsular War veteran of whom Lord Uxbridge, commanding the cavalry at the time, had remarked, 'Bacon is, without doubt, the best cavalry officer I have ever seen.' Major Bacon, knowing he would never command the regiment under the financial terms that existed, went off to take service as a mercenary with the King of Portugal. The system was driving competent but poor officers out of the army.

Yet the purchase of commissions had been a rule for over 170 years. Up to the Napoleonic Wars it had worked well, and often led the British to victory. The system might sound crazy, but behind it lay sound reasoning.

Earlier in their history, the English people had sampled a military dictatorship, and never wanted another. Towards the end of Oliver Cromwell's life, his major generals had governed the country like petty local dictators, interfering exasperatingly in private life – abolishing mince pies and Christmas and maypoles – to such a degree that ordinary folk had gone to cheer and dance in the street when Cromwell died and the King was restored.

Never again did England want an army officered by military adventurers. The political philosopher Edmund Burke expressed the general opinion when he declared, 'An armed, disciplined force is, in its essence, dangerous to liberty.' The system in operation since 1683, of purchasing army commissions, meant that only men of property could become officers. The money they paid was a guarantee for their good behaviour.

But, in recent years, railway building and industrial development had poured enormous sums into the pockets of the landowners who, traditionally, officered the army. So, as the rich got richer, the sums changing hands for important commissions in fashionable regiments became so huge as to exclude the poor officer who knew his job from all but the lowest ranks of the service. He remained a lieutenant or captain, and did the donkey work.

Lord Lucan, at fifty-four, was the youngest of the British generals commanding. He was full of nervous energy, and had a passion for looking into every trivial detail himself. He was an obstinate man, irritable and proud, but was exceptional among his contemporaries in having seen active service. In 1828, he had served on the staff of a Russian brigade commander, in a war against the Turks in the Danube provinces. Lucan might have made a competent lieutenant or captain. He wanted always to be in the thick of the fighting. Even those who liked him least would admit, 'He's brave, damn him.'

Lord Lucan's bitterness came, in part, from relishing authority, yet being, inwardly, aware that he was not quite equal to the responsibility with which he had been entrusted. Recalled from retirement on his Irish estates to command the cavalry in the Crimea, Lord Lucan began badly, on his first parade. He intended to show off his men's paces to the Turkish commander-in-chief, but it was seventeen years since Lord Lucan had served with the cavalry, and, since his day, the words of command had been changed. A few misunderstood orders threw the 5th Dragoon Guards into spectacular public confusion. That sort of thing is long remembered against an officer, by the men serving under him.

Lucan never clearly understood Lord Raglan's reasons for keeping his precious cavalry – the eyes of his army – 'in a bandbox', during the march down the coast to the walls of Sebastopol, instead of throwing them away in gallant battle charges and pursuits where they were certain to be outnumbered.

On the eve of Alma, Lord Raglan had been obliged to send his most senior staff officer to prevent Lucan from charging a Russian cavalry reconnaissance that outnumbered him two to one. Without cavalry, the allied army would march blindly; this must never be risked. During the battle itself, a thousand British horsemen had faced four thousand Russian cavalry, without stirring from where they stood. This was in strict obedience to Lord Raglan's orders, though cavalry officers who did not know the reason why implored Lucan to 'let them come on'.

Around him, Lord Lucan began to hear whispered his new nickname, 'Lord Look-On' – though he was 'looking-on' only because Lord Raglan had ordered him to. The fact rankled bitterly.

After Alma, Raglan once again had sent three successive orders forbidding a headlong pursuit when the Russians were in full retreat. So the cold public rebuke after Lucan got lost on the flank march went home like a blow. Lord Raglan was known to have told his cronies that he thought the cavalry was being 'wretchedly handled'. From the flank march onward, as if stupefied with resentment, Lord Lucan began to carry out all orders reaching him from above with a marked lack of enthusiasm.

The British army's new base, south of Sebastopol, was at Balaclava Bay, where, by 9 October, all the men not on front-line duty were under canvas. This small deep-water inlet, which the navy liked because ships could be brought close inshore, had for the army two serious drawbacks. Only a very efficient supply system could have kept all the munitions and supplies needed by the entire army briskly on the move through such a small port. The British army's supply system was hopelessly antiquated – so Balaclava Bay soon became a bottleneck.

Moreover, it was six or seven miles away from the British sector of the front. This long line of supply was vulnerable to Russian attack. Now, once an army is cut off from its base, it is soon helpless. The French, up the coast, drew their supplies through two spacious bays, called Kamiesh and Kazatch, nearer their front-line troops, and less vulnerable to Russian attack.

As you went inland from Balaclava, you reached a plain shaped like a bowl, two miles wide by three across. The bowl was intersected by a hog's back of high ground, so as to form two valleys. Farther inland still, where a plateau intersected with ravines rose six or seven hundred feet, the British lines around the south-east of Sebastopol had been established. The track from Balaclava Bay up to the British positions on the Heights of Inkerman was now the lifeline of the British army.

Five sixths of the British who landed had managed to

reach Balaclava, but of these, 25,000 men, nine out of ten, were suffering from diarrhoea. Though the army was dwindling visibly from sickness, it yet remained an effective fighting force, highly disciplined, and splendidly confident after its victory at Alma.

Prince Menshikov, somewhere inland, commanded an army larger by far than the British, and had already received 12,000 fresh men. Down the long roads from all over Russia, as if drawn to a magnet, reinforcements were marching south to increase his numerical strength.

The last plan of Sebastopol in British hands had been drawn by Colonel Mackintosh in 1835 – nearly twenty years before – but not much had changed. The new gun emplacements mounted by Colonel Todleben might exact their price from the attackers, but still, in the Colonel's own opinion, could not withstand assault. Until the last days of September the Russians were still pessimistically expecting the allies to take the city at the point of the bayonet.

But Lord Raglan, elderly, cautious, diplomatic, once again felt that he could not act without his allies. General Canrobert, new to command and a political general, was well aware that what Louis Napoleon's precarious dictatorship needed most was a spectacular and cheap victory. An assault on a fortified city, that had not been softened up by a heavy bombardment, might lead to a depressingly long French casualty list. And what if the bold venture failed?

Yielding to his allies, Lord Raglan announced that the siege train, of heavy guns, must be landed from the ships offshore. Until then – for another three weeks – his army must patiently wait.

His chief engineer was slow, systematic, seventy-two-year-old Sir John Burgoyne, who had served against the Americans at the siege of New Orleans forty-two years before. His hair standing up all over his head, as usual, Sir John solemnly agreed that heavy guns were essential. 'Land the siege train!' raged General Cathcart, commanding the

Fourth Division. 'But, my dear Lord Raglan, what the devil is there to knock down?'

General Cathcart had been named in the Dormant Commission to succeed Lord Raglan if the British commander became a casualty. But so far, Lord Raglan had ignored the advice of the man named to succeed him – as he was ignoring it now. Carthcart was becoming another resentful general.

By the start of the formal bombardment, on 17 October Sebastopol was much stronger than it had been in mid-September. The Russians had been hauling whole broadsides of naval guns ashore, and mounting them in hastily dug earth batteries. They had hundreds of guns to draw on, from their dismantled warships as well as the naval arsenal. Moreover, the allies had not properly invested Sebastopol – drawn a tight cordon around it, so that no men or supplies could move in or out. The Russians, therefore, had by now been able to send all the civilians safely out of the city.

On 6 October they had brought in 25,000 troops to reinforce the garrison, which, by then, numbered 5,250 soldiers, 5,000 workmen, and 25,600 seamen and marines landed from the fleet.

At dawn on 17 October, smoke rose from the biggest artillery duel that, until that day, the world had ever seen and heard. The starting signal was the firing of guns from three French mortars at 6.50 a.m. By dusk, the allied guns had fired off nine thousand projectiles – shot and shell. The Russians had replied with a grand total of twenty thousand. Once that day the allies were gratified to see dust and rubble fly volcanically upward. This was a sign that they had exploded a magazine in the Redan – one of the Russians' main bastions – and killed a hundred men there at one stroke. The guns in the ominous Malakoff Redoubt were also silenced, and brave Admiral Kornilov was mortally wounded there. But it was also observed that the Russian naval gunners could fire off their broadsides faster and more accurately than the allied artillerymen.

Colonel Todleben expected the bombardment to be followed by assault – near dusk, as he admitted later, the defence was paralysed. But once again the French, handicapped by an explosion in their main magazine on Mount Rodolph, hung back. Colonel Todleben's men worked all night, with heroic and frenzied zeal, to repair the damaged parapets and mount fresh guns from the huge store in the naval arsenal.

By the morning of the eighteenth, the Russian gun emplacements silenced in the previous day's bombardment were firing on the allies once more. After all that hail of shot and shell, Sebastopol was as strong as ever. The bombardment had killed over one thousand Russians – but thousands more, in their long grey coats, with their brassbound muskets, were streaming across the roads of the Ukraine to reinforce the army in the Crimea.

By early November the Russian army in the Crimea numbered 120,000 men, or more than double the force of the allies. Colonel Todleben went on vigorously to complete, under the eyes of the besieging allies, his scientifically planned circle of defences. And winter was coming on.

The Indian summer came to an end. The last day of October brought north-east winds and bitter frost.

'My best generals', said Tsar Nicholas, 'are General January and General February.'

The first use the Russian army made of its enhanced strength had been to come down from the inland heights and cross the plain of Balaclava, with the intention of cutting the British off from their base of seaborne supply.

Hidden in scrub woodland across the valley of the river Tchernaya, the Russians under their celebrated General Liprandi had assembled a force of 22,000 infantry, 3,400 cavalry, and 78 guns. At dawn on 25 October 1854 they moved down unexpectedly into the valley of Balaclava, and began to attack, in force, the port's outermost defences – a row of sketchy earthworks dug along the hog's back intersecting the valley, where nine 12-pounders were mounted, manned by a garrison of 1,100 Turks.

The nearest support for the beleaguered Turks was in the harbour of Balaclava, nearly two miles off. The main Turkish strong point was an earthwork on Canrobert Hill, which the Russians bombarded with 30 guns, and stormed with 5 battalions. Outnumbered more than ten to one, the Turks fought gallantly. One hundred and seventy died where they stood – half the Turkish force had become casualties before the survivors fled.

The British cavalry – now strengthened by the landing of the Heavy Brigade, under its Brigadier, James Scarlett – was standing to its horses an hour before dawn. Lord Lucan, now commanding all the British cavalry, had made himself unpopular by giving the order for this dawn stand-to, but the strictness of his drill was today abundantly justified. The troopers saw the point. As, holding their horses' heads, they heard gunfire from the Turkish redoubt on Canrobert Hill, they were ready to meet what was coming down on them.

In the way of the huge Russian army, as it moved out of the hills towards the vital supply ships crowded into Balaclava Bay, stood only 550 Highlanders, under Sir Colin Campbell, along with 100 invalids, a handful of Turks – and the British cavalry, thinned out by disease, which so far in this war had never had a chance to distinguish itself.

Lord Raglan himself, whose headquarters were six miles inland, had come with his staff across the heights, and from his vantage point, 700 feet above the undulating valley of Balaclava, was able to observe all the details of the action clearly, as in a theatre. The view of his senior officers, who were actually taking part in the battle down there, was often obscured by smoke or rising ground.

Lord Raglan could see that Lord Lucan's cavalry, awkwardly placed, was within a musket shot of the now occupied Turkish redoubts, and in the line of fire of the Highlanders. Slowly they were withdrawn along the southern valley, on Sir Colin Campbell's urgent advice, to a position where the British cavalry would threaten the Russians' flank as they moved towards the sea.

Lord Raglan would have liked to march down his infantry and fight an infantry engagement but a certain caution was justified. There was always the possibility that this attack on his lines of communication might be a feint to distract attention from a mass breakout from Sebastopol. He ordered the 4th Division of Infantry down into the plain.

General Cathcart refused at first to move his men, claiming they were exhausted. Not until ten that morning did the infantry begin to move. The delay put a tremendous responsibility on the cavalry, and that handful of Highlanders.

About 4,000 Russian cavalry, to begin with hidden from Lord Lucan by the lie of the land but visible to Lord Raglan, were slowly moving across the north valley towards the British positions. Their horse artillery opened up on Campbell's Highlanders, lying down under the gunfire in a line two men deep – all that stood at this moment between the Russians and the sea.

'Men – remember!' Sir Colin Campbell shouted. 'There is no retreat from here. You must die where you stand!'

On the word of command, up sprang his 550 Highlanders, and fired a tellingly accurate volley into the dense and overwhelming mass of enemy cavalry. And a second volley. Though ludicrously outnumbered, the thin red line held firm.

Seeing this handful, like a fringe of skirmishers, so boldly block their way to Balaclava, the Russians hesitated, as if fearing a trap. Surely, behind this handful of kilted Highlanders must lie hidden some much more formidable force, waiting in ambush? When the advancing Russians wavered, the Highlanders, exalted with delight, would have charged with the broadsword, but Campbell's ringing voice checked them: 'Ninety-third! Ninety-third! Damn all that eagerness!' At a third volley from the Highlanders of the 93rd Regiment, the Russian mass wheeled and withdrew.

A handful of men had held back an army.

Though Lord Raglan's orders had taken half an hour to come down from the plateau, he had got the Heavy Brigade moving. Eight squadrons under Brigadier-General Scarlett suddenly found themselves riding across the front of a vast mass of mounted Russians only a few hundred yards off. The Heavy Brigade, diminished by sickness, comprised men of the 5th Dragoon Guards, Inniskillings, and Scots Greys, with the 4th Dragoons and Royals slightly to the rear – a total of 500 sabres. The nearby Russian cavalry outnumbered them at least eight to one.

James Scarlett, a stout, red-faced man with a large white moustache and thick, good-natured eyebrows, was fifty-five. Though he had seen no active service personally, he had wisely chosen as his aides-de-camp in the Crimea two experienced officers who had taken part in recent cavalry warfare in India. When Scarlett saw that relentless mass of Russian cavalry come down on him, he at once took it for granted that his paltry eight squadrons would attack. He wheeled his five hundred horsemen into line with a smile.

Scarlett handled his men with meticulous care, as if this were simply another morning on the parade ground. All those long hours of gruelling drill at last became justified. On one flank, his troopers were obstructed by the remains of a ruined vineyard – fallen walls, tangled roots, hidden holes. Deliberately, though the mass of Russians a few hundred yards off were also forming line, Scarlett ordered his squadrons to take ground to the left, and thereby step clear of the obstruction. The next need was to dress his frail double line of horsemen until each was as straight as a ruler's edge.

The Russian trumpets meantime blew. The Russian line advanced at a measured trot, downhill, towards the hopelessly outnumbered British.

While the ominous mass of grey-clad cavalry came on, Scarlett's junior officers were laboriously dressing the British front line of 300 sabres, moving horsemen a few feet back and forth until the line was impeccably straight. The Heavy Brigade had so far remained stock still, while the Russians with raised swords came down on them, to push them aside and get to the sea. The deliberation, the cold confidence of the British evolutions, all carried out as if on parade, were beginning to shake Russian morale. Why, the Russians again wondered, should this handful of men act so suicidally? Did those eight squadrons mask some trap?

Last-minute doubts like these prompted the Russian commander to make a serious tactical error. Russian trumpets sounded the order to halt. From the Russians' massive central square, horsemen were thrown out in two wings, to outflank the British entirely.

Here was a wonderful chance for audacity. Cavalry should always try to receive a charge from enemy cavalry when in movement, since horsemen receiving an onset at the halt sustain a greater shock. Scarlett gave the order to charge.

Ever since they had ridden side by side in a famous cavalry engagement at Waterloo, a tradition of friendship had existed between Greys and Inniskillings. Again they went headlong at the foe, side by side, sabres raised, uttering their awe-inspiring battle cries – the wild Irish yell of the Inniskillings, and, from the Greys, a deeper, growling moan.

James Scarlett, fifty yards ahead of his men, plunged with uplifted sword amid the Russian horsemen. Lord Raglan and his staff, watching anxiously from the heights, could see the first British line of 300 men disappear into the vast grey mass like drops of blood – and bob up again, here and there, as a circle of foes penning them in compelled the British to make a space for themselves with merciless sweeps of the sabre.

They found those long Russian greycoats were thick enough to turn the edge of a sword – and that Russian shakos could hardly be split with a hatchet. So it was, 'Strike at their faces, boys!' In that mêlée there was only hand-to-hand fighting, no firearms, all cold steel. Inniskillings and

Dragoons of the second British line had by now smitten the Russian mass on the left, and the charging Royals were making their impact on the right. Submerged in grey those red-coated British swordsmen might be, but it was becoming plain to the watchers on the heights that, under the stress of this hand-to-hand fighting, the Russian cavalry mass was losing its formation.

At the very moment when the Russians seemed to be shifting their ground, perhaps cracking, Lord Lucan ordered the 4th Dragoon Guards to charge. This final blow was perfectly timed. The Dragoons went thundering through the disordered Russian mass from one flank to the other. The Russian cavalry had already begun to break up, and turn in retreat. The threat to Balaclava Bay was, for the moment, over.

When Lord Raglan sent his personal word of praise to the general commanding the Heavy Brigade, 'Well done, Scarlett!', the bloodstained cavalrymen around their Brigadier, under the stress of it all, burst into tears. The Charge of the Heavy Brigade had, for once, enabled British cavalry to show the best they had – the outstanding bravery of the officers, the perfect discipline and steady courage of the men.

So far this day the Light Brigade had taken no part in the action. They now had a splendid chance to pursue the retreating Russian horsemen, once the Heavies had broken their ranks. Instead they let them cross the hog's back to take up a new position at the end of the northern valley. When Lord Cardigan, commanding the Light Horse, was ordered in pursuit, he refused. Cardigan had been ordered, earlier in the day, to hold his present position, and as far as Lord Cardigan was concerned, that was that.

4

Into the Valley of Death

FOR twelve days prior to the battle of Balaclava (25 October) Lord Cardigan, commanding the Light Brigade, had avoided the discomforts of life under canvas by living aboard his private yacht, *Dryad*, which had recently arrived in Balaclava Bay with his French chef on board. Irreverent junior officers who were cheerfully sharing the hardships of their men began to call him 'The Noble Yachtsman'.

Lord Cardigan was not loved. An irritable man of limited intelligence, a fanatic on the minor details of drill and discipline, and obsessed by fears that other officers were intriguing against him, he had risen to the rank of major-general in the army largely by the luck of having been born heir to an earldom and £40,000 a year. His family said that Lord Cardigan's nature had never been what it once was since as a boy he fell from the saddle on to his head. A military historian who knew him well in the Crimea described him, charitably, as 'innocent as a horse'. Few others had a good word to say for him.

Cardigan's first regimental command (achieved a mere eight years after joining the cavalry in the lowest commissioned rank, as a cornet of horse) had been of the 15th Hussars, for the lieutenant-colonelcy of which he was reputed to have paid between £35,000 and £40,000. He replaced a good-natured and efficient professional officer, Colonel Thackwell, who had seen service in Spain and at Waterloo. Lord Cardigan began to run his regiment obsessively, like a martinet – as if the men under his command were toy soldiers, given him to dress up according to his private fancy, and arrange in neat patterns for his own amusement.

54

His behaviour to his brother officers became so high-handed, neurotic, and outrageous that, in the end, after a succession of ugly scandals, Lord Cardigan was expelled from the command of the 15th Hussars. To drive the lesson home, the order demoting him was read at the head of every regiment in the service.

One might suppose such a public rebuff would bring Lord Cardigan's military career to a dead stop. Yet, through court intrigue and backstairs influence, he managed, not long after, to buy the lieutenant-colonelcy of the 11th Light Dragoons for £40,000. There was, of course, a public outcry; but since it happened to be led, in Parliament, by a radical called Molesworth, who was not only critical of the army as such but known to be in favour of abolishing flogging (then thought essential for keeping discipline), a majority of 280 members of Parliament loyally rallied to defend the British army – little as they might like Lord Cardigan personally.

When asked his opinion of Lord Cardigan's professional competence, Lord Lucan (who also happened to be Cardigan's brother-in-law) was heard to remark, 'He is not fit to have charge of an escort.' Between the two noble lords there was no love lost. Cardigan always did his best to balk at the orders of his brother-in-law, Lucan, now his immediate military superior. The refusal to follow up the Charge of the Heavy Brigade by a light cavalry pursuit was typical of the man.

Lord Lucan himself, since that public rebuff for losing his men on the flank march, had hardly been on speaking terms himself with Lord Raglan, his commander-in-chief. These conflicts of personality among the generals were brewing up disaster.

Lord Cardigan had been in the custom of spending a quarter of his income – £10,000 a year – on enhancing the appearance of the 11th Light Dragoons. He dressed them in skintight cherry-coloured trousers, employed an excellent London tailor to make them jackets of royal blue edged with gold, gave them fur-trimmed pelisses with bullion braid and gold lace, and topped them off with high-plumed fur hats. But there was more to service in Lord Cardigan's regiment than all this dressing up. In the first six months of his command, Lord Cardigan held fifty-four courts-martial. In one month alone, there were eight courts-martial, and a hundred defaulters.

Two later scandals put Lord Cardigan's second regimental command in jeopardy, but, each time, he was saved by his superiors' unwillingness to let politicans interfere with the army. Cardigan was, to begin with, arrested and tried by his peers in the House of Lords for having duelled with an officer he had unjustly driven out of his regiment. He was acquitted, thanks to a technicality, but it was discovered that he had fought the duel with rifled pistols fired by a hair trigger – which seemed murderous rather than gentlemanly or sporting. Then, on Easter Day 1841, he had a soldier of his regiment flogged after church, on the very spot where the religious service had just been held. There was another public outcry, yet Lord Cardigan lived it down.

This was the man, obtuse to the point of stupidity, irritable almost to the pitch of madness – yet, as he was soon to prove, certainly no coward – who now commanded the Light Brigade. He knew cavalry drill perfectly, and was himself a superb horseman, but Major-General the Earl of Cardigan entirely lacked the true instincts of a cavalry leader – the faculty for taking in an entire situation at a glance, the gift for acting with bold initiative.

The Light Brigade, which had numbered a thousand sabres when it landed at Calamita Bay, was now reduced by sickness to 636 men. After the charge of the Heavy Brigade had compelled the Russian cavalry to withdraw in turmoil, the Light Horse were deployed so as to look down the long, narrow north end of Balaclava Valley, like a corridor walled by low hills, at the end of which now glared a battery of twelve Russian guns. To the right were those three earth redoubts, including Canrobert Hill, which the Russians had taken from the Turks, each mounting eighteen-pounders. The hills to right and left were grey with Russian infantry.

A mile and a half away, at the end of the narrow valley, in support of those 12 guns that now confronted the Light Brigade, the retreating Russian cavalry had halted, and turned to form three lines, each of over 1,000 men.

All this was clear to Lord Raglan, from his vantage point 700 feet above the battlefield. But in framing the necessary orders for his army, the British commander was doubly handicapped.

After nearly thirty years as an administrator behind a desk, where tact was needed more often than forthrightness, Lord Raglan had learned to avoid putting his orders into clear, bleak words that might allow of only one interpretation. And from his active service as a staff officer, many years before, he remembered how often the situation on a battlefield can change between the time an order is given, and the moment when it must be obeyed. Raglan's inclination, therefore, was to avoid giving an order which allowed no option to the man on the spot.

It had also got to be known that General Airey – energetic, confident, sometimes over-optimistic – who acted as Raglan's chief of staff without formally having that rank, would sometimes issue an order in the name of the commander-in-chief. This left plenty of scope, for any subordinate who so chose, to doubt if any particular order might have come from Raglan himself, and even to quibble about what it might mean. Lord Raglan, in short, left too much to the good sense and professional ability of the men serving under him, when often just these qualities were lacking.

Moreover, he lacked a reliable and well-trained staff to make his intentions clear to his field commanders. Aristocratic favouritism was commonplace. Five of Lord Raglan's staff officers happened also to be his own nephews. Of the 221 officers comprising the staff of the entire expeditionary force, only fifteen had been through the Senior Department of the Royal Military College at Sandhurst. All the others were untrained in their special duties.

After carefully inspecting the battlefield below, Lord Raglan decided that the Russians were shaken by their two rebuffs, from the Highlanders and the Heavy Brigade, and had begun to waver. He framed an order encouraging his commanders down there in the field to follow up this advantage. These were the words he wrote:

Cavalry to advance, and take advantage of any opportunity to recover the heights. They will be supported by infantry, which have been ordered to advance on two fronts.

(But which heights? The cavalry down there had heights both to left and right. And where were the promised infantry?)

The infantry mentioned in this order were, in the main, those whom General Cathcart had been unenthusiastic about getting on the move. They would arrive too late on the battlefield to play their intended part.

Lord Lucan, though well aware his subordinates were restive for action, and critical of his caution, took this order to mean, literally, what it said: that he should lead his cavalry forward only when properly supported by infantry. To take this view was strictly in accordance with the book. Cavalry lost their effectiveness, in a battlefield situation, when they acted without infantry support, not least in attacking enemy guns, when infantrymen should be close at hand, to hold firmly what the dash of the men on horseback might temporarily seize. Moreover, had not Lord Raglan, from the very start of this campaign, kept his cavalry 'in a band-box'?

This time, though, Raglan, seeing the battlefield situation clearly, actually wanted to risk his precious cavalry. A dash at those earth redoubts, which the Turks had yielded, might now recapture them. And there was another important consideration. Lord Raglan could see that the Russians had brought horses and lasso tackle to the redoubts, and were hauling away the British naval eighteen-pounders which had been mounted there. In the Russian capital, St Petersburg, the arrival of captured British guns would be taken as evidence of a victory. And by now in this war, the Russians needed some kind of victory, even a fictitious one, to stimulate morale.

Rapidly Lord Raglan dictated to General Airey yet another order – his fourth in succession.

Lord Raglan wishes the cavalry to advance rapidly to the front, follow the enemy, and try to prevent the enemy taking away the guns. Troop Horse Artillery may accompany. French cavalry is on your left. Immediate.

(*Wishes*, not *orders*. What *front*? The Light Brigade could see enemies on three sides at once. And this, the vital and final order, would arrive in the handwriting of General Airey, mistrusted by the army as prone, on occasion, to put words in his master's mouth.)

Captain Lewis Nolan, in the forage cap and tiger-skin saddle cover of his regiment, the 15th Hussars, pushed his way forward, and begged urgently to be allowed to take this order to the cavalry commanders in the valley below. Lord Raglan consented. Nolan, an officer with highly developed opinions about the proper use of cavalry in war, was perhaps the best horseman in an army of magnificent horsemen. He urged his charger forward, to make his way down a precipitous track where it seemed to onlookers no horse could pass – bearing the order to the battlefield more quickly than any of the staff officers would have thought feasible.

Yet choosing Captain Nolan as his messenger was Lord Raglan's last and fatal touch, unconsciously completing the tragedy that was preparing under all their eyes.

Captain Nolan, an excitable enthusiast, was the expert advocate of a system for the bold use of cavalry in warfare. Over the past few weeks, he had shown a dangerous contempt for Lords Lucan and Cardigan as commanders. Cavalry, in his professional view, must be used with a boldness that at times may seem reckless if it is to have its best effect. After one cavalry skirmish, only a fortnight before, Captain Nolan had accused Lord Lucan to his face of neglecting his duty. Here in the Crimea chances had again and again been lost, in Captain Nolan's opinion, because of the hesitation, the incompetence of Lord Look-On and the Noble Yachtsman.

Today, in those successive written orders, Lord Raglan had shown that at last he was willing to risk his cavalry. Yet the horsemen down there on the plain, whom Nolan was breathlessly approaching at full gallop, stood in line, immobile. Captain Nolan knew that the order he was carrying downhill at breakneck speed would get them going. They were to attack. Lord Raglan's last words, shouted to Nolan as he rode off, had been, '*Tell Lord Lucan the cavalry is to attack immediately.*'

Lord Lucan, down on the plain, could not in fact see that the Russians were towing off British eighteen-pounders as trophies of war. He had not kept close watch on the enemy positions, nor made a reconnaissance. As far as events on the battlefield went, Lucan knew only what happened under his very eyes.

Captain Nolan, on his lathered charger, rode up to Lord Lucan with a certain insolence and delivered the commander-in-chief's order. Lucan's dark-complexioned face grew even darker. In angry perplexity he asked the messenger, 'Where are we to advance to?'

Theatrically, Captain Nolan swept an arm towards the foe. In a voice touched with contempt, he said, 'There are your enemy, my lord. There are the guns.' But the guns towards which his outflung arm happened to point were those staring down from the very end of the valley, later named by the poet Tennyson 'The Valley of Death' – that battery of twelve Russian guns, which had thousands of Russian cavalry massed in its support.

Captain Nolan wheeled his horse off quietly, and joined his friend Morris of the 17th Lancers. He now had what he wanted: a chance to take part in this cavalry charge Lord Raglan had ordered.

Lord Lucan, though sometimes slow off the mark, had an accurate, literal mind. Simply to ignore these confusing orders was, in the first place, out of the question. Had not the great Duke of Wellington laid it down that, on the field of battle, orders conveyed by an aide-de-camp, whatever his rank, even someone as detested as Captain Nolan, must yet be as rigorously obeyed as if uttered by the commander-in-chief in person?

Lucan could also remember, as he saw those Russian guns a mile and a half away stare back at him, how often in this campaign he had been reproached simply for obeying Lord Raglan's frequent orders to keep his men in hand. By checking their aggressiveness he had become unjustly despised. Now, cavalry charges were evidently coming into fashion.

The general officer commanding the Light Brigade was, anyway, his opinionated and pigheaded brother-in-law, Lord Cardigan. All I am doing, Lord Lucan reminded himself, as he informed Lord Cardigan what was expected of him, is simply passing on Lord Raglan's order.

'Certainly, sir,' Lord Cardigan replied. (*There are your enemy. There are the guns.*) 'But allow me to point out to you that the Russians have a battery in the valley on our front, and batteries and riflemen on both sides.'

'I know it,' Lucan replied coldly. 'But Lord Raglan will have it. We have no choice but to obey.'

Lord Cardigan took personal command of the first line, which, he ordered, should comprise the 13th Light Dragoons, the 17th Lancers, and the 11th Hussars. The second line, which also included the 4th Light Dragoons and most of the 8th Hussars, was commanded by Lord George Paget.

Cigars, that traditional solace of the crack cavalry officer, were becoming rather scarce in the Crimea. Lord George Paget, as orders were given to charge the Russian battery, had just lighted one that was large and particularly choice.

Was it consistent with a senior officer's dignity to go into action with a cigar between his lips? He struggled manfully, but had not the heart to throw his cigar away after a couple of puffs. Throughout the desperate action that followed, Lord George Paget was to be observed riding against the foe with smoke coming out of his mouth.

The officers of the Light Brigade had begun once more to dress their men's lines with parade-ground exactness as if for a royal review. The officers of Lord Cardigan's personal staff rode three lengths ahead of the first line of troopers, and took up their position. Of the staff's many wartime privileges, not the least was that of getting to grips with the enemy first.

Lord Cardigan himself rode out in advance, alone, two lengths ahead even of his staff, and as he rode was heard to observe, in a rather bored voice, 'Well, here goes the last of the Brudenells.' King Charles II had raised a loyal old cavalier officer named Brudenell to the peerage in 1661, as Earl of Cardigan. The present earl was the last of his line. And now, about to charge those guns, he confidently expected to be killed.

Lord Cardigan drew his sword, and, in quiet tones, declared, 'The Brigade will advance. Walk, march, trot.'

The Heavy Brigade, meanwhile, was forming behind the Light Brigade, to support their attack; the Horse Artillery, however, had to be left in the rear, because part of the valley was ploughed land. The fire of those Russian guns would therefore not be answered.

The mile-wide valley was a deadly three-sided trap. On Lord Cardigan's left, ranged along the Fedioukine Hills, which marked the valley's northern boundary, were eight battalions of enemy infantry, four squadrons of cavalry, and fourteen Russian guns. On the hog's back, heights to Lord Cardigan's right, where the Turks had once been, were eleven enemy battalions, some of them sharpshooters, armed with a newly imported Belgian rifle, as well as field batteries and thirty heavier guns. At the far end, as the Light Brigade moved forward, now came into view that mass of Russian cavalry, drawn up in their three lines, with twelve guns un-limbered before them, and three lancer squadrons on each flank. Concentrated on the valley floor in such a three-way cross-fire, the Russian shot and shell, musketry and rifle fusillade could tear to shreds any living target that dare move across that open space.

As the Light Brigade began deliberately to walk their horses in the direction of death, there was a strange, brief hush across the entire battlefield, broken only by the jingle of bits and accoutrements. Cholera and dysentery had already cut into their numbers: the 17th Lancers and 13th Light Dragoons were led, at this moment, by mere captains. But, shrunk down though the formations might be, they were still, in their bearing and drill, the finest light cavalry in Europe, disciplined to perfection.

This, too, was the one great moment of Lord Cardigan's lifetime, the only occasion when he would need, not brains, which he sadly lacked, but sheer animal courage, which he possessed in abundance. As Lord Raglan admitted after-wards, 'He had the heart of a lion.'

Cardigan was now riding quietly at the trot, his back erect, sword held high, never turning in the saddle. During a charge, a cavalry officer, like a runner, must control himself never to glance over his shoulder – a backward glance dis-courages the men behind. He was immensely conspicuous in his bizarre uniform of cherry red and royal blue, worn with a gold-laced pelisse. Trotting forward astride his bloodstock chestnut charger, Ronald, as if man and horse were one, Lord Cardigan virtually alone led the way for his Brigade into the Valley of Death.

For the first fifty yards, as they trotted through this in-credulous hush, the troopers following Cardigan could not be sure whether his objective might be those captured British guns on high ground to the right, which they could see the Russians towing away – or the battery of twelve enemy guns at the end of the Valley.

The Russians, as Cardigan rode into the Valley, could hardly credit the evidence of their own eyes. On the captured redoubts most exposed to attack, the Russian infantry were already forming hollow squares – the correct formation to repel cavalry. But the British were riding in a quite different direction – on to certain death.

When the Russians opened fire from three sides at once, and still the steady trot continued, straight down the Valley, everyone knew for sure.

Captain Nolan was quick to see the misunderstanding. From his front-line place with the 17th Lancers, he galloped wildly forward. His charger crossed obliquely the solemnly advancing line. He wheeled round at full gallop in front of Lord Cardigan himself – a gross breach of etiquette.

Nolan was waving his own sword, shouting loud and urgent words – but what he had to say was drowned by the roar of Russian guns. The enemy gunners now had the range. A shell exploded close to the solitary shouting rider. Fragments tore open his breast, and exposed to all the sight of Captain Nolan's beating heart.

In a weird and dreadful agony, sword arm stiffly erect, screaming an unearthly cry, Captain Nolan galloped back the way he had come, riding as if in uncontrollable despair right through the ranks of the Brigade, like a portent.

Lord Cardigan up to now had taken all this coolly. From that moment on, he became enraged. His blood was up. The threat from the Russian guns had not made any great impression on his mind; but the vile manners shown by Captain Nolan in riding across his commanding general's front, and, above all, that wild, uncontrolled, almost girlish scream, were two things Cardigan simply couldn't ignore. As he later admitted, all that occupied his mind during the charge was anger against Captain Nolan.

The French were stupefied. Watching the British troops' slow and ceremonious advance under merciless cross fire – an advance in parade-ground precision – General Bosquet exclaimed, *'C'est magnifique, mais ce n'est pas la guerre'* (It's splendid, but it isn't war), a remark soon to become a catch phrase. But Bosquet had his wits about him. To relieve the ordeal of his allies, he sent orders to the Chasseurs d'Afrique, experienced French troopers riding Algerian horses and used to attacks over rough country. They began bravely engaging the Russian troops along the Fedioukine Hills, to Cardigan's left.

Though, behind his stiff ramrod of a back, the cannonade was tearing holes in their ranks, Lord Cardigan still held his brigade under absolute command. When a direct hit knocked out man or horse, or ploughed its way down an entire rank, the survivors would move up impassively, correctly, as if at daily drill, to form the rigid line anew. But even the most iron discipline could not hold flesh and blood at that slow trot for ever. Cardigan had, once, to check with a wave of his hand the impatient captain commanding the inner squadron of the 17th Lancers, who might otherwise have trotted his men forward, out of line. The only words of rebuke Cardigan spoke, during the entire advance, were, '*Steady, steady, the Seventeenth Lancers.*'

Into the zone of shot and shell now rode the Heavy Brigade. They were some way behind the light horse because their regulation pace was slower. Lord Lucan had been hit in the leg, and staff officers around him were wounded. By now the Light Brigade, under the spur of that terrible bombardment, quickened their pace to a canter as they approached the Russian guns. They were so clearly pulling away from the Heavy Brigade that Lucan ordered a halt.

He turned the Heavies to take them out of range of the Russian guns – 'in order,' as he explained later, 'to protect the Light Cavalry against pursuit, on their return.'

By now, the Chasseurs d'Afrique were vigorously engaged on the Fedioukine Hills. The fire from that flank was slackening, and, in the course of the action, fell silent.

The Light Brigade was in a headlong gallop at last, the chargers still in line having been excited out of all control by riderless troop horses breaking loose in a panic. A cavalry charger with a trooper on its back will continue to advance in formation even though wounded. Riderless, it runs wild. The Brigade's second line had, meanwhile, advanced at the trot for nearly a mile, picking its way through the British dead.

At last, came the shouted order, 'Close in! Close in! Close in to the centre! Close in! Close in!'

At eighty yards, the Russians fired a salvo from their twelve guns, point blank at the oncoming horsemen. Of the Brigade's first line, only fifty men remained, and by now were fighting around the guns. Lord Cardigan himself had been the first man into the Russian battery.

The second line came up, led by Lord George Paget, who was still smoking his cigar. They took the Russian guns headlong, sabreing the gunners – took Russian guns that they could not possibly hope to hold.

The commander of the Cossack lancers covering the Russian guns, Prince Radzivill, recognized Lord Cardigan, whom he had once met at a ball in London. His Cossacks were given orders to capture the British Major-General alive. But Lord Cardigan had no wish to spend the rest of the campaign as a prisoner of war – under conditions perhaps less agreeable than those aboard the yacht *Dryad*. As he later explained, in his opinion it was 'no part of a general's duty to fight the enemy among private soldiers'. He evaded the Cossacks, and began to ride back down the Valley, slowly, under fire, alone, a solitary target, returning the way he had come.

Having, in his own words, 'led the Brigade, and launched it with due impetus,' Lord Cardigan considered his duty done. He rode his chestnut, Ronald, back almost at a walk, brooding deeply – not about the loss of his Brigade, or the shot and shell and sharpshooters' conical rifle bullets that fell profusely about him, but about the strange, the grossly ill-bred, the utterly unpardonable behaviour of Captain Nolan.

When, out of the enemy's range at last, Lord Cardigan

encountered James Scarlett of the Heavy Brigade, the first words that exploded from him were, 'Imagine the fellow – screaming like a woman when he was hit!' To which Brigadier Scarlett made the dignified, the chiding reply, 'Say no more, my lord; you have just ridden over Captain Nolan's body.'

Not aware that their general had already left the field, the survivors of the Charge of the Light Brigade, under Lord George Paget, still had a grim mile to go on the return journey. The retreat was worse than the advance. All formation was lost. Wounded men and bleeding horses made their way blindly through a tornado of shot and shell. The charge had taken eight minutes; the fighting around the Russian guns, and the return, took another twelve. But to the 70 men who lived unscathed to complete the charge, it must have been an eternity. Another 125 eventually came in wounded. The 17th Lancers had been reduced to 37 troopers. The Light Dragoons now comprised two officers, and eight mounted men.

As they one by one reached safety, Lord Cardigan, as if at last contrite, said to the survivors, 'Men, it is a mad-brained trick, but it is no fault of mine.' To which his troopers are reputed to have given the answer, 'Never mind, my lord, we are ready to go again.' They probably did; they probably were. That was their style.

One Lancer called Wightman, who had been wounded four times, was taken prisoner, and brought in front of the Russian General Liprandi, who asked him, 'What did they give you to drink? Did they not prime you with spirits, to come down and attack us in such a mad manner?'

'You think we were drunk?' Private Wightman answered the Russian general. 'My God, I tell you, if we had so much as smelled the barrel, we should have taken half Russia by this time.'

Lord Cardigan, impervious to practically everything, returned to his yacht, had a bath, and went comfortably to bed after a bottle of champagne and a good dinner.

Lord Lucan, who always shared the discomforts of his men, and who cheerfully boasted on one occasion of being as lousy as they were, loudly denied Lord Raglan's angry accusation that he had 'lost the Light Brigade'.

'I gave the order to charge under what I considered,' said Lord Lucan, 'a most imperious necessity, and I will not bear one particle of the blame.'

Where, indeed, did the blame for the tragic blunder lie? On an elderly commander-in-chief who always did his conscientious best, but who had lost, after years of paper shuffling, the accurate, urgent habits of war? On a system of purchasing commissions that was part of the national tradition, and had worked well in the past? On General Cathcart's slowness off the mark? On the lack of a trained staff? On Lord Raglan's ambiguously worded orders? On Lord Lucan's blindly literal interpretation of them? On Lord Cardigan's obstinacy? On Captain Nolan's error of judgement, for which he paid with his life?

The Russians, anyway, were never able, then or after, to break the British line of supply from their entrenchments around Sebastopol to their base at Balaclava Bay. From the day of this battle onward, however, the Russians straddled the only good hard-surfaced road. Front and base were now connected merely by a country track, which soon would be deep in mud. Five hundred cavalry chargers had been lost in the Valley of Death; thousands of pack animals had been left behind in Bulgaria. Winter would soon be upon them and as the churned-up mud became deeper, the vital line of communication linking Balaclava to the British trenches was to fray away to a mere thread.

5

Mud and Muddle

THE nineteenth century was the great time of scientific discovery and technical achievement. With the Minié rifle and the steam-driven warship, as with the shell which exploded on impact instead of bouncing along like a ball, had come the first signs that science was about to transform warfare.

Another recent invention – the electric telegraph – was to make a big difference in this war. The outcome of a battle now became known in London or Paris not when the dispatch rider arrived on horseback, but at the speed of light. Therefore, politicians for the first time could interfere rapidly in the workings of the war machine.

In old-time wars, no one had known or cared how the common soldier fared, or how hard he died. During the Napoleonic wars, entire British armies had been wiped out by incompetence or disease – for example on the ill-fated Walcheren Expedition, where some Crimean officers had served as young men. Yet, in those days, no civilian knew why. This was to change. Along with the electric telegraph, there appeared a new man with a new trade on the field of battle, the war correspondent.

The Times was the most powerful paper in Britain because it represented a new breed of men, who had made their money in manufacture and trade, rather than from the ownership of land. Efficiency and common sense and low taxation appealed to the hearts of men like these far more than military glory. *The Times*, knowing its readers both detested the Tsar as a tyrant, and feared for the safety of the route to India, had begun by welcoming this conflict. Yet its correspondent in the Crimea, a thirty-four-year-old Irishman called W. H. Russell, was now beginning to criticize trenchantly the way the generals were running the war. As the scandals he exposed came to light, the daily thundering of *The Times* began to shake the British government.

William Howard Russell had known hard times himself as a boy in Dublin, where his father had failed in business. Sent to Trinity College, Dublin, at his grandfather's expense, he had been obliged to drop out before taking his degree. He had gone to London to read law, but was thirty before being called to the Bar. Meanwhile, he managed to support himself by doing odd jobs of journalism. Delane of *The Times* noted his talent for vivid yet exact reporting, and his knack of getting to the right place at the right time, and when war broke out, sent him to the Crimea. There, Russell had an important effect on the course of the war.

Not only did Russell report the battles as an eyewitness – so that the peaceful British merchant at his breakfast table could thrill to the ardours and agonies of the Light Brigade before putting on his frock coat and making his way soberly to the counting house. Russell also recounted, and for the first time, the personal heroism and the unnecessary sufferings of the ordinary British soldier.

In mid November, after the crisp, bright autumn weather in the Crimea had turned to rain and wind and cold, there was not much fighting to write home about. One day Russell sent off a descriptive story of a great storm that had hit the British camp in Balaclava Bay and played havoc with the shipping there.

Nearly one half of our cavalry horses broke loose. The wounded had to bear the inclemency of the weather as best they could. Lord Lucan was seen, sitting up to his knees in sludge amid the wreck of his establishment. Lord Cardigan was sick on board his yacht in the harbour of Balaclava, in all the horrors of that dreadful scene at sea.

Towards twelve o'clock, the wind became much colder. Sleet fell at first, then came a snow storm, which clothed the desolate landscape in white, till the tramp of men seamed it with trails of black mud.

At the narrow neck of the harbour, two or three large boats were lying, driven inland. The shores were lined with trusses of hay, which floated out of the wrecks, outside the harbour.

That storm, which wrecked twenty-one ships offshore, and crippled eight others, was soon to take the blame for killing off the British army in the Crimea. By January 1855 only two months after the storm, Russell was obliged to write home:

One of the most melancholy subjects for reflection in the world was the sight of our own army. It consisted of officers, men and regiments almost new to this campaign. The generation of six months before had passed away.

On 7 January 1855 the 63rd Regiment had only seven men fit for duty. The Scots Fusilier Guards, who had come out to the Crimea 1,562 strong, could muster only 210 men on parade. The British army, in two months of winter, had, as it were, faded and fallen into the mud of the Crimea. It was estimated that of every 100 men in battalions serving at the front who died that winter, 73 were dead as a consequence of hunger and lack of clothing – and this when Britain was the richest country in the world, and possessed a fleet in the Black Sea twice as large as the French, by means of which the army could have been amply supplied.

Because of the electric telegraph, cruel facts like these could no longer be hidden from the breakfast tables of tax-payers at home, who had the votes and paid the bills. As the roar of civilian indignation rose, the politicians knew they would have to put things right.

The official army view of how the British Crimean army had been lost was simple and logical and had the additional advantage of leaving every high-ranking officer and army institution free of blame.

An army of close to 60,000 men had melted away, simply for lack of those bales of fodder that Russell saw washed up on the narrow shores of Balaclava Bay after the big storm.

The Commission of Enquiry's ingenious argument ran as follows:

In one of the wrecked ships was a three-week supply of fodder for the army's chargers and pack animals. Fodder, to an army dependent on animals for transport, is obviously as vital as petrol is to a modern motorized army. For three weeks after the storm, therefore, those horses couldn't be fed. They died off faster than they could be buried. Now the presence of large numbers of putrefying animal carcasses is not exactly healthy – is there any wonder that sickness in the army grew? Blame fodder.

Meanwhile, the men in the front line had to be supplied daily with rations and munitions of war. Since the Battle of Balaclava, supplies had to be taken up a single track, knee-deep in mud. Every day 112 tons of supplies were needed, which normally would represent a load for 2,000 pack animals.

But since the pack animals were dying off – for lack of fodder – shot, shell, powder, meat, and biscuits had to be carried by the soldiers themselves. This harsh extra duty meant, of course, that more of them fell sick. Next day there would be fewer soldiers still to carry up necessary supplies, therefore each fit man would have a greater weight to carry. Still more would fall sick.

And why, you might end by asking, are the British sick and wounded carried off so much more slowly to the hospital ships than are the French? The French, of course, have horse ambulances, the French have comfortable tents, dry dugouts, a surfaced road, rations of tobacco and brandy. But then, the French have fodder for their horses. It all comes back to fodder.

W. H. Russell and others, however, were quick to point out a flaw in this ingenious and seemingly watertight story.

The Royal Navy happened to have sent ashore a naval brigade, to man the ships' guns now taking their share in the bombardment of Sebastopol. The naval ratings were sharing

the duties and risks of their front-line army comrades. They
endured the same wearisome alternation of frost and thaw,
the same mud.

They ran the same risk of disease, on a terrain where carcasses and corpses were unburied for lack of fit men to dig
graves – where, in the waters of Balaclava Bay, floated
dozens of amputated human limbs, pitched there hurriedly
by surgeons to save the bother of burying them. Despite all
this risk of infection, the death rate among the navy men ran
at $10\frac{1}{2}$ per cent, of which 7 per cent was from fatal wounds;
whereas the average army death rate among soldiers employed carrying stores was 24 per cent, among infantrymen
at the front was 39 per cent, and in the most exposed and
distant entrenchments ran as high as 73 per cent. The essential reason was evidently not lack of fodder. What made the
difference?

Naval officers, when they collided with regulations that
kept them from getting new boots and dry clothes for their
men, would club together and buy such necessities out of
their own pockets. The sailors had cooked food and proper
sanitation. As they came off duty at the guns, their wet
clothes were at once taken from them, and they were given
warm dry clothes to put on. They slept, not in mud, but
under cover. They drank, not from cholera-infected puddles,
but water as safe as precaution could make it.

Lord Raglan was gentlemanly and compassionate. Why
should he have let such things happen to his army?

Raglan had some notion where the fault lay. He had more
than once politely and unsensationally written to London,
requesting that improvements be made in the Commissariat
and its systems of supply. Old for a commander when the
campaign began, he was seen to age perceptibly as the
dismal winter continued. He too, like his soldiers, was a
victim of the crazy way the British army was admin-
istered.

Wrote W. H. Russell:

Lord Raglan went out to one or other of the Divisions every day he could spare from his desk. Perhaps there was no clerk in England who had as much writing to get through as the Field Marshal in charge of the forces. I believe his lordship was frequently up till 2 or 3 o'clock in the morning, looking over papers, signing documents, and exhausting his energies in secretary's work.

Every officer from the commander-in-chief downward was kept busy signing forms. The bureaucratic system in which the British army had become entangled was almost unbelievable. It had been designed, through the long years of peace, to save the taxpayer's money by deliberately making the issue of stores difficult, so that the army would cost as little as possible.

Lord Raglan's immediate military superior, the Commander-in-Chief of the British Army, an old Waterloo veteran called Lord Hardinge, did not in fact command the whole army from his office at the Horse Guards in London. He had no control whatever over two essential branches of it – the Royal Artillery and the Royal Engineers. He had no control over the supply of weapons, either. He could order a court-martial, but he could not transport or feed his own troops.

The Master General of the Ordnance, who controlled artillery and engineers, also supplied all the men in the army with muskets, and provided their greatcoats. Not their uniforms. Only their greatcoats.

The political control of the army was also split up ingeniously, to make the dodging of responsibility easier than the taking of firm decisions. There were two separate Ministers: the Secretary at War and the Secretary of State for War, each with different functions. The Secretary at War, so called, could give no order to the army, but he controlled military finances. He did not, however, feed the army. The Commissariat, which did buy food for the army, as well as arrange its transport, was under the Treasury, and therefore controlled directly by the British Prime Minister. But though the Commissariat bought essential supplies, the Purveyor, an entirely distinct office, actually gave them out as they were needed.

To get any clerk in any one of these conflicting departments to act in the most trivial matter involved a mountain of requisitions and receipts. The clerks were too busy, anyway; there were not enough clerks to go round. The army's entire medical department had a staff of twelve clerks. The sixty-four-year-old Commissary General for the Army of the Crimea could call on the services of only three clerks. The Purveyor, a man seventy years old, had been given two clerks and three messengers to organize the feeding of 60,000 men. Most of the time they were crushed to immobility under a mountain of forms they could never hope to get properly completed.

Those who suffered worst from this system were the men in the trenches, but the difference now was this. For the first time in British history, thanks to W. H. Russell and the electric telegraph, the public knew.

Plenty of excuses were offered. The men, said some, were obviously being killed by the notorious and terrible Russian climate. But the Crimea is far to the south, and its climate, though changeable, is no worse than that of the north of England. The British army before Sebastopol was destroyed that winter not by Russian frost or Russian guns, but by the British themselves.

Not until as late as 8 November 1854, so Russell discovered, had Lord Raglan told Mr Filder, his Commissary General, to make provision for the army's wintering in the Crimea. By November, all hope of taking Sebastopol by quick assault had clearly failed. On 14 November, came the great storm that dashed twenty-one vessels to pieces. What better excuse would an old man like Filder want, who had been suddenly called upon to do the impossible? Whenever anything was urgently needed for the army, it was to be found, of course, in one of the ships that had been sunk. Too bad.

*

The British soldiers in the trenches slept without cover from the weather, and never took off their boots. They were usually under fire, either from Russian shells, or from the sharpshooters holed up in rifle pits, which Colonel Todleben had sent out to defend his perimeter. Basic shipboard rations of salt pork and ship's biscuit did, however, generally reach them.

The men in the trenches had already begun to suffer badly from frostbite. Now, after living exclusively on shipboard rations for months – food that contained no vitamins – they began, as did sailors on voyages long ago, to suffer from scurvy.

Yet, seven miles away, as Russell was quick to point out, Balaclava Bay was full of vegetables. One entire ship's cargo, of cauliflowers, had been thrown into the water because the correct papers to permit them to land could not be found. In store at Balaclava were warm clothes; there were rice and flour, tea and coffee, even coal. Seven miles away, up a muddy track, the troops had frostbite and scurvy. When one day, by lucky chance, a ration of coffee did reach the front line, the beans were green – unroasted and unground, and there was no fuel to cook them on, anyway.

The animals suffered along with the men. By the end of November, artillery camps were already being invaded by a horde of ravenous cavalry horses, thin as skeletons, which would break loose from their pickets and gallop whinnying into the camp at the sound of the feeding trumpet – a bugle call they all knew – there to seize fodder from the very mouths of the artillery horses. By the end of the year, most of those chargers were dead.

The French despised the British, for, although as soldiers they knew how to fight, they were ignorant about how to look after themselves in the field. The French had larger harbours nearer to their lines, and could supply their troops over paved roads. Their men had some protection in the tents that each squad of three men shared. French infantrymen spent one night on trench duty, one night resting. So, while the British army dwindled, the French, because of their system of conscription, were able to draw on large reserves of trained manpower. Their numbers grew from 45,000 in October to 65,000 in December. The British not only lost men, they lost influence. From now on, this was going to be preponderantly a French war – which meant, in fact, that an ambitious dictator called Louis Napoleon, in Paris, would use the electric telegraph to interfere more and more directly with the decisions of the soldiers in the field.

The direct interference sparked off in the British army by Russell's dispatches was, however, all to the good. An attempt at building a paved road from Balaclava Bay to the front line failed because the Turkish labourers working on it died off quicker than they could be replaced. But, by January, work was begun on a railway, nicknamed 'The Grand Crimean Railway with Branch to Sebastopol' which went three miles over hard rock up a height of 630 feet – a serious feat of engineering at the time. This was the first instance of railways playing a significant role in warfare. From the beginning of history until 1855, armies had moved at the pace of man and beast. Now, war was to be mechanized.

Patriotic people in Britain began collecting money and comforts for the army in the Crimea. Furs, mufflers, flannel shirts, pious tracts, preserved meats, potted game, drink, and tobacco were sent on their way across the Mediterranean – but the men who enjoyed these comforts were usually raw recruits, sent to replace those fighting men whose earlier sufferings had stimulated public sympathy. Huts, tents, and warm clothing were needed fast – contractors supplying them notoriously made handsome fortunes. The war was losing its popularity, at least with the rich. It had more than doubled the tax on unearned income. That was a high price to pay, even for glory.

By 13 February 1855, when the schooner *Erminia* of the Royal Yacht Squadron sailed into the crowded anchorage at Balaclava, skippered by Lord Ellesmere and loaded to the gunwales with the first of the comforts purchased by the

Crimean Armies Fund – flannel shirts, pocket combs, bottled ale and the rest – the hardest of the privations were over, and, anyway, spring was near.

Midwinter, however, had been terrible, as one set of figures alone will show.

By 22 January 1855, a total of 60,000 British soldiers had been sent to the Crimea. On that date, only 17,000 men were fit for active service. Of the 43,000 men dead, sick, or wounded, only 7,000 had been disabled by the enemy. All the others were the victims of mud and muddle and disease.

Next day, 23 January 1855, a lawyer called Roebuck, a member of Parliament with an incisive intelligence and a bleak integrity, got up to speak in the House of Commons. He was a little man who wore black, with a parsonical white neckcloth. He was an ardent reformer, and had the reputation of being a radical. Crippled, sweating with pain, he rose to move 'for a Select Committee of the House to inquire into the conduct of the Army before Sebastopol, and the Departments of Government concerned'.

Roebuck's speech was devastating and unanswerable. The motion was carried, the Secretary at War resigned, and in the political tidal wave that followed, Lord Aberdeen, believed to have been half-hearted in his efforts for the war, was replaced by Lord Palmerston. Parliament's Select Committee, with Roebuck as chairman, began with remorseless thoroughness to extract simple facts that put an end to all the excuses.

Thus, at a time when the entire British army was supposed to be falling to pieces for lack of fodder, a ship called the *Tynemouth*, loaded with grain, was sailing to and fro from Balaclava to Scutari and back again, never being unloaded because the paperwork involved had not been sorted out. Even when fodder did arrive, cavalry horses, starving in their horse lines, had not, at one critical moment, been sent the short distance to Balaclava Bay to eat their fill, and carry more fodder still back to camp, because of 'a difficulty in obtaining the signing of receipts'. Men and beasts had died by the thousands because official forms lacked signatures.

General January and General February betrayed Tsar Nicholas at the last. They may have played havoc with his foes, the British – but they killed their own master.

The Tsar had been hard hit by the war's first Russian defeat. If thirty years of drill and discipline couldn't hold Russia together, then what hope was there? The Tsar took to his bed, a nervous crisis developed, and from then on the imperial autocrat who liked to play with toy soldiers was never himself again.

Nor was Russia. Under the Tsar's imposed façade of automatic obedience, much in the great country's political organization was proving to be rotten. But the Russians lacked such democratic institutions as a Parliament, which might, at the moment of crisis, have given effect to the people's will. The hollow fraud of the Tsar's drilled and obedient Russia was beginning to crack and crumble as the long winter roads leading from all parts of the Russian empire to Sebastopol began to whiten with the bones of Russian conscripts. Two out of three Russian soldiers died from hunger, exposure, or neglect on their long winter march to the Crimea.

At the end of February 1855 Tsar Nicholas himself caught a chill while inspecting the drill of his palace guard on a frozen parade ground in the bitter heart of the Russian winter. On 2 March he died. No one yet had any reason to dislike his successor, Tsar Alexander II, who indeed had the reputation of being somewhat of a liberal.

6

The Fighting in the Fog

AT the onset of the winter of 1854, the Russians learned, through their spies, how feebly held was the British sector of the front.

Badly fed, incompetently handled, beginning to be reduced by privation and disease, the British army was in Russian eyes a fighting force of rapidly dwindling effectiveness. The French might be growing stronger, but the British were on the downgrade. Could such men as they now were withstand a massed Russian push to the sea?

The entrenchments, which the British had so far managed to dig in the thin, rocky soil along their front line, posed no serious obstacle. The most vulnerable point in the British position was the left flank, where the Second Division had been pushed dangerously far forward towards the heights of Inkerman – cliffs of yellow stone honeycombed with caves and intersected by ravines that ran down to the Tchernaya River. Yet, by early November, this entire division had managed to throw up merely a single sandbag battery on the hill confronting Inkerman. As yet, there were not even any guns in the battery. The men in the front line there, like all British soldiers still capable of standing on their two feet, were being worked to death as pack animals.

Early on the morning of 5 November 1854, a foggy Sunday obscured by drizzle, the sound of wagon wheels was distinctly heard by sentries nearest the Russian lines. Many men in the exposed advanced posts held by the Second Division had been on duty without sleep for over forty-eight hours. The division lacked men even for duties vital for keeping a grip on their sector of the front. They sent no patrols out into no-man's-land. No pickets had been sent forward to probe Russian intentions and watch for an attack. The men of the British Second Division had been wholly occupied with keeping warm, keeping awake, keeping alive.

Their commanding officer, Lieutenant-General de Lacy Evans, a conscientious old Peninsular War veteran, had been sending the commander-in-chief urgent warnings about his division's exposed state. But he was now sick on board ship, like so many of his men.

At 5.30 a.m., in the hour before dawn, when human vitality is at its lowest ebb, the Russians in their long grey overcoats fixed their sword bayonets and moved forward through the fog towards the British lines. Major-General John Pennefather, an exuberant Irishman commanding the first brigade of de Lacy's division, at once took command. He was young, as Crimean senior officers went – only fifty-four. Ten years before, during the Sind campaign, he had led a battalion of Irishmen in the Battle of Miani, when 2,000 men under Sir Charles Napier, only 500 of them Europeans, beat an Indian army of 35,000 strong. Pennefather was unlikely to lack faith in his men, or to be over-impressed by the odds against him.

He knew, though, to a nicety, the weakness of the British position. His division had a remnant of 3,000 men in the line – highly disciplined soldiers who had withstood disease and exposure and were still capable of obedience and willing service. Three-quarters of a mile down the mud track to his rear was his nearest reserve, the Brigade of Guards, the elite corps of the British army, six-footers wearing huge bearskin caps. Perhaps 1,300 Guards would still be fit enough to march into action.

The Russians, in overwhelming numbers, were already coming down on the British through the thick weather. There was no time, and little scope, either, for the tactical dispositions of scientific warfare – for the British soldiers were short of ammunition, besides being ludicrously outnumbered.

Pennefather made up his mind, therefore, to send his entire division now reduced by disease to only 3,000 men (compared with 16,000 in the average Russian division) against the foe piecemeal, in small formations as they came up ready to fight. The British were sent out into the fog with bayonets lowered, to fight to the death with whatever Russians they came up against. It was a desperate, reckless, amateur battle plan, against all the rules, and it succeeded in confusing the Russians utterly. The fog hid what might lie behind Pennefather's men. The Russians supposed they had run against a fringe of outlying British skirmishers, obstinate fighters and hard to shift – who must, according to the rule of war, mask a large army, somewhere close behind, and poised to strike. They had no idea, at first, that the skirmishers were the army, and that behind them lay nothing.

A young Russian officer who spoke French and English was employed during the siege of Sebastopol to interrogate some British prisoners, men from the ranks. He was amazed to find how intelligent, confident, and good-natured they were. Most of them had a clear idea of why the war was being fought. A fair number knew how to read and write, and some were even in the habit of reading the newspapers and of forming political views.

The Russian soldier, by contrast, though he had many fine qualities, was only dimly becoming conscious of his rights as a human being. His sufferings in this war were to give him a more distinct idea of what those rights might be. The notion had even begun to germinate, in the minds of Russian frontline soldiers, that, since they had shown themselves no less men than their officers, serfdom should be abolished.

The sum total that a young Russian conscript knew of the world, when he left home to join the army, was what he might have heard from the lips of the priest, in a village which he could never legally leave without the consent of his nobleman, and where he himself would be sold, along with the cattle and the manor house, should the estate ever change hands.

To the unthinking Russian peasant, put into a grey uniform and drilled in the mechanical responses necessary for a soldier, this was simply a holy war. He knew he was led by the Tsar – a royal personage of a power semi-divine, before whom, as he could easily observe, the strongest in the land bowed down their heads. The Tsar had assured his people that his quarrel with the Turks – who were Muslims – was simply over his undoubted right to protect from persecution the Orthodox Christians living in the Turkish Empire. The Tsar had publicly asserted, 'Russia fights not for the things of this world, but for the Faith. England and France have ranged themselves on the side of the enemies of Christianity, against Russia, fighting for the Orthodox Faith.' This was what the pious Russian peasants believed when they went to war.

Hidden from view on the honeycombed plateau above the British positions, 35,000 of these simple but vigorous Russian soldiers had been crowded. (There was space to deploy effectively perhaps half that number.) They were supported by 134 guns, of which 54 were of heavy calibre. The entire Russian army, heavily reinforced, now numbered 100,000 men.

Before moving out to battle, the troops had been reviewed by two young Grand Dukes, Michael and Nicholas, personal representatives of the Tsar, and partaking in his semi-divine power, who, the soldiers were told, had come to the Crimea to share in some of the hardships, ardours, and glories of the siege. The Russian soldiers had also been blessed by the bearded priests of their church. The church bell had rung loudly in their ears as they marched away. Moreover, before going into action, they had all been liberally dosed with vodka. Their special orders were to kill enemy officers wherever they saw them, whether mounted or on foot.

The British officers, many still in their gaudy parade-uniforms, some still wearing gold epaulettes, were conspicuous on the battlefield. However, when Russian officers wore their greatcoats, they were distinguishable from their men only by a thin gold stripe on the shoulder. To the Russian mind it seemed logical that the British common soldier, once his officer had been shot, would not know whom to obey or what to do, and would simply lay down his arms.

In fact, most of the troops Pennefather had been sending forward, in formations up to company strength, with orders to get to grips with the advancing Russians, had but the vaguest idea who their superior officer might be, or what was the chain of command. The men themselves could often scarcely see beyond the tips of their bayonets. If, when there was a gap in the fog, the British soldiers saw Russian grey ahead, they raised a hurrah, fired off what ammunition they might have left, and, when the pouch was empty, charged headlong with cold steel.

General Soimonov, commanding the first Russian attack, had sent forward skirmishers of his own – 300 sharpshooters with rifles. The advantage the British had enjoyed at Alma, thanks to the accuracy and penetrative power of their Minié rifles, was a wasting asset. Many of the Russians attacking in the first wave were armed with Liège double-grooved rifles, though the bulk of the army still carried muskets.

On behind their skirmishers came the Russian first line – 6,000 men strong, with 3,300 in support. Backing them up was a general reserve of 9,000 infantry with 16 field guns. Before the Guards arrived, therefore, each British soldier in the Second Division might have to cope with six Russians.

There were flashes of rifle fire through the fog, and wild shouts. A drizzle of rain came down unendingly. Fighting was fiercest around Sandbag Battery – a symbolic strong point for which both sides contended ferociously, though in fact it held no guns. The British infantry manning Sandbag Battery had long since fired off all their ammunition. They were now holding off the Russians by stabbing with bayonets, or clubbing with their rifle butts. Some threw stones at the foe. One British soldier, whose rifle had been wrenched from him, was seen in a fighting rage using his fists to knock down his Russian antagonist, and then kicking him to death. The rank-and-file British soldiers had no love to spare for the Russians, who were in the habit, after an engagement, of systematically bayoneting the enemy wounded, under the orders of their officers – like serfs hoeing a field.

In the valley, which the Russians were now attempting to cross, the main British line of defence was a wall of loose stones, called the Barrier. As a barricade it was trivial, but, in this confused hand-to-hand fighting, it was something to group around and contend for. The Russians had begun by advancing in their usual massed columns a battalion strong – but soon they lost formation over the open ground. When sent on in company columns, they were at times reduced to a disorderly mob – vodka and parade-ground precision did not go together.

The right wing of the Russian advance, colliding with men of the British 49th Regiment, had been struck by a volley that tore gaps in their grey-clad ranks. They were driven back the way they had come, at the point of the bayonet. General Soimonov now led 9,000 of his men against the British left and centre. Meanwhile, hidden beyond the British left flank, in a deep chasm called Careenage Ravine, which drove a natural wedge into the front, a column of Russian soldiers was moving up. This column was to outflank the British left unexpectedly, and go on to encircle completely the small British force holding up the Russian advance.

Meanwhile, at the warning rumble of dawn gunfire, every unit in the British lines still capable of combat was hurrying into action, to reduce the desperate odds now pressing on the Second Division. In the nick of time, as the Russian soldiers were about to emerge threateningly from the mouth of their ravine, there arrived 650 men of the Light Division, supported by a field battery, which strengthened the British left. At this stage in the battle, Pennefather had 3,600 to hold the Russian attack, and 18 field guns – which, admittedly, were left ineffective and unsupported on a ridge, under heavy enemy bombardment.

General Buller and 650 men of the 77th Regiment were also marching through the lifting fog towards the sound of the fighting. They came on the scene at the very moment when the outflanking force of Russian soldiers many times their number broke cover from Careenage Ravine.

'There are the Russians, General – what shall we do?' asked Colonel Egerton.

'Charge them!' was Buller's instant reply.

The 77th Regiment ran at the Russian soldiers with lowered bayonets, while a company of the Guards, who had also come up fast and moved in to bear the brunt of the fighting, managed to hold the Russian flanking force in a cross-fire from the opposite side of the ravine. The outflanking manoeuvre was checked. General Buller was wounded by a ball that killed his horse. General Soimonov had been killed at the head of his men.

This, after all, was the sort of fighting in which the British army excelled. From the officers, no special tactical skill or professional finesse were demanded, only courage, and they had plenty of that. Inkerman was a battlefield situation that could be saved only by the magnificent fighting qualities of the common soldiers, sharing the risks with regimental officers they knew and trusted.

General Pavlov now took command, deploying nine battalions opposite the British right, at Sandbag Battery. Four of these Russian battalions – about 3,000 men – marched on the Barrier, defended by 200 British soldiers of the 30th Regiment with their fixed bayonets.

These British soldiers charged the two leading enemy battalions, who outnumbered them on the field about seven to one. After hand-to-hand fighting of unbelievable ferocity, the two leading Russian columns were driven back on the two columns moving up to their support. All four Russian battalions withdrew from the field in disarray.

A thin red line comprising 525 men of the British 41st

Regiment led by their brigadier, Adams, formed in extended order on the higher ground of Fore Ridge. They opened a systematic fire on General Pavlov's remaining five Russian battalions, massed below – numbering nearly 4,000 men. Then they charged down the hill at them, driving the Russians back to the River Tchernaya. The battle, so far, had been one of quantity against quality, where masses of conscripts were pitted against highly trained soldiers, not only able to form line and keep in step amid the bloody chaos of battle, but also of such natural aggressiveness that, once they got to grips with their enemy, almost nothing on earth could withstand them.

The attack had begun before daybreak, at 5.30 a.m. Two hours later, at 7.30 a.m., a balance could be struck across this wild, disordered battlefield. The Russians had, so far, advanced 15,000 men across a terrain where the British, opposing them, had no entrenchments or fortifications to speak of, except Sandbag Battery and one loose stone wall, the Barrier. The Russians had been repulsed by a force that they overwhelmingly outnumbered, their dense columns having been torn up by rifle fire from the less vulnerable British two-deep line, and they had been driven back in disorder by cold steel. The British still had a slight superiority in weapons, since only a minority of the Russians were armed with the new Belgian rifles, whereas only the British 4th Division still carried muskets. In the artillery duels, however, which had gone on as an endlessly resonant and deafening counterpoint to the hand-to-hand fighting, the Russian guns had generally been superior, and often had silenced the British.

Though the first Russian attack had been heroically held, this sort of fighting, against such odds, could not go on forever. The Russians were now combining General Soimonov's reserves with the battalions under General Pavlov, which had just been driven from the field. For their next attack, the Russians were able to assemble 16,000 fresh troops on Mount Inkerman, supported by 96 guns.

Meanwhile, on the British side, during this brief lull in the battle, privates could here and there be seen, under the crash of an enemy cannonade, falling asleep where they stood – bone tired after forty-eight hours on guard and two hours of fighting for their lives.

Sergeant Timothy Gowing, of the Royal Fusiliers, had received bayonet wounds in both thighs during this action. Bearing in mind the Russians' nasty habit of killing Allied wounded, he was lucky to get off the field alive. He later gave his personal impressions of the battle of Inkerman in a few vivid and convincing phrases:

As many of us as our General could spare were ordered to march, as fast as our legs could carry us, to the assistance of our comrades, then at the dreadful fight raging at Inkerman. Our blood was up, but we were hungry – many of us had had nothing to eat for twenty-four hours, and we were wet through to the skin.

Well, to the fight we went, and the sights were something horrible, but there was not a desponding voice. The fog was so dense that we could not see twenty yards. The determined rushes of the Muscovites were hurled back, time after time. Their princes boasted that they would drive us all into the sea; so they would, perhaps, if weight of numbers could have done it, but that nasty piece of cold steel stood in the way.

The queen of weapons [the bayonet] was used with deadly effect – the drunken, massive columns of the enemy were pitched over the rocks by men who might die, but never surrender. The odds were heavy, but, from the brutes we had to face, we had no mercy to expect. A mere handful of Britons were contending for their very existence, for to be beaten meant an ignominious death at the hands of a host of fierce brutes, mad with drink – Dutch courage had to be poured into them, to make them face our ranks. We had no supports or reserves, but every man, as soon as he could reach the field, went straight at them, with a shout which seemed to strike terror into them. And so the fight went on, hour after hour. It was as well that the French came up when they did. Our men were gradually being crushed.

The Russians launched a new assault at the British centre, with 10,000 men, supported by an effective cannonade.

More British were by now coming up. General Cathcart had reached the battlefield, with 2,100 men of the Fourth Division. The Guards were already heavily engaged.

The Russians came on in such numbers that at first they outflanked the Barrier, obliging the British infantrymen ranged along the stone wall there to fall back or be surrounded. But detachments of the 21st and 63rd Regiments, with the Rifle Brigade not far behind, came rapidly up to sustain them, and together they managed to drive the Russians back with cold steel.

Bitter fighting still went on between the five hundred or so British under Brigadier Adams, who had been holding Fore Ridge overlooking Careenage Ravine against the attack of eight times as many Russians. It was near here that General Cathcart made his name in the battle, and met his death.

Sir George Cathcart, at sixty years of age, was a disappointed man. Perhaps of all the senior army officers of aristocratic descent in the Army of the Crimea (he was a son of the Earl of Cathcart), Sir George took his professional responsibilities most seriously. He had not only taken part in the great European battles at the end of the Napoleonic era, but had written an interesting military study of them. In an army where most general officers had not heard a shot fired in anger for half a lifetime, Sir George Cathcart came to the Crimea fresh from two successful wars against Bantu tribesmen at the Cape of Good Hope.

Yet, on the day of Alma, his division, the Fourth, had been left in reserve, and was not even engaged in the fighting. Twice on the march he had been left commanding the rear-guard. Lord Raglan continued to take little notice of the Dormant Commission, which, since it named Cathcart to succeed in the command, should also, he supposed, have warranted his opinion being taken on questions of strategy. But, Lord Raglan openly preferred to confide in his old Peninsula cronies, like Generals Burgoyne and Brown.

When the army arrived before Sebastopol, after the flank march, Cathcart had gone out of his way to advise Raglan to storm the place at once. In the light of what we now know, from Russian sources, of Sebastopol's unpreparedness, this was sound advice, and might have saved the army the horrors of a winter at Balaclava. On 4 October, a month before the Battle of Inkerman, General Cathcart had incautiously addressed to Lord Raglan a letter, protesting about the influence that General Airey and General Sir George Brown had acquired over the destinies of the army, and alluding, perhaps tactlessly, to the Dormant Commission.

Raglan's answer was frigid – and nine days later arrived a letter from the Secretary of State for War, cancelling Cathcart's Dormant Commission, and, hence, his right to succeed in command. Cathcart took this, reasonably enough, as a slight on his professional capacities – perhaps even on his courage – and now was nagged by a fear that this might be what the whole army had begun to believe.

He could never forget that at the Battle of Balaclava, on 25 October, he had been slow, perhaps wilfully slow, in bringing up his men. Had the infantry of the Fourth Division arrived in time to support the Light Brigade, the wasteful tragedy of the Valley of Death might never have occurred.

On the morning of Inkerman, halfway through the battle, Sir George Cathcart arrived headlong on the field with his first brigade, having hurried towards the firing determined to act in a way that would wipe out any slur on his honour.

Major-General the Duke of Cambridge, commanding the Guards, asked Sir George Cathcart to fill up a gap on the Guards' left. The Duke, a cousin of Queen Victoria, had for a few months been heir presumptive to the British throne, although he began his military career as an officer in the Hanoverian Army.

The Duke was a brave, modest, and competent soldier. At Alma, the first time in his life under fire, he had valiantly led the Guards in person, and now, on the day of Inkerman, the

Duke brought his men up rapidly and threw them into the thick of the action. When his horse was shot from under him, the Duke, singled out as a fine target by Russian sharpshooters, might have fallen on the field, had not a regimental surgeon of the 7th Hussars, who in fact had no business doing the work of an infantry subaltern, led a handful of Guardsmen in a charge, to rout the Russians.

Cathcart took up the position he was asked to fill on the Duke's left; but he kept searching the scene of battle for a chance to distinguish himself personally.

Lord Raglan by now had reached the battlefield, and was trying to pierce the smoke-filled fog and make sense of what might be happening. Raglan began by telling Pennefather he would be left to direct the fight without interference. This news was greeted with a radiant smile, and a bellow of Irish oaths aimed at newcomers who needed direction through the confusing fog. But Raglan wanted, tactfully, to restore some order to the British line, which, if made coherent, would be stronger than if new arrivals continued to be sent up against the Russians piecemeal, in small groups. Raglan must also have had a shrewd idea what was passing through Cathcart's mind, because he took immediate steps to check his impetuosity.

He sent an order by General Airey, who acted as his chief of staff, the officer of whom Cathcart had already formally complained. The order that General Airey, this time with the authority of Lord Raglan himself, bore to General Cathcart, was that 'he should move to the left, and support the Brigade of Guards, and not descend, or leave the plateau'.

There is some dispute as to whether this order actually reached Sir George Cathcart. Probably it did, and, in the state to which his mind had been wrought, might well have seemed yet one more jealous attempt to prevent his distinguishing himself. In either event, Lord Raglan's judgement of the probabilities was correct.

When Cathcart had originally inquired of Pennefather where he wanted the men of the Fourth Division, Pennefather had answered, with an Irish exuberance that simplified the tactical problem enormously, 'Everywhere!' To Sir George Cathcart it now seemed that in front of his very eyes a magnificent tactical opportunity was developing. A Russian column, marching up the ravine in front of the British position, had begun to menace the Guards, who already were in danger of being cut off. But what if a small British detachment went forward, and took them by surprise in the flank?

This would mean, of course, leaving the plateau. But General Cathcart was in no mood to take anything into account that might stand between himself and death or glory.

He sent four hundred of his men downhill to the right of the Guards' position, thus creating a hole in the line, and took command of them to attack the extreme left of the Russian column. A sudden attack delivered audaciously with such a handful against the compact, onward-marching Russians might, indeed, have stood a chance of success, granted the advantages of surprise, and of firepower. The men of Cathcart's Fourth Division, however, were armed only with muskets. They made their way downhill without greatcoats, conspicuous in their scarlet jackets with white crossed bands. They were admirable targets for Russian riflemen, and Sir George Cathcart himself, on his Arab horse, wearing the plumes of a divisional general, was the most splendid target of all.

Moreover, the gap now created in the British line had horribly exposed the Guards' flank. Already a Russian column was forcing its way through this gap, so as to outflank and isolate the Guards, some of whom were following Cathcart's men downhill; while others, after firing off their ammunition, were compelled to fight their way out of the encirclement with the bayonet.

Cathcart, in a desperate last attempt to remedy his blunder, and to ease this pressure on the Guards, rallied fifty men of the 20th Regiment, to lead them in a frenzied and futile charge uphill. In the moment before he was shot down dead from his horse, his last words to his favourite staff officer, Lord Maitland, were, 'I fear we are in a mess.' Perhaps Lord Raglan's private opinion about the military talents of his designated successor was right, after all.

Luckily, the French had begun to arrive. Two French battalions had been sent by General Bosquet, to reinforce the British right, though they came up rather sluggishly. Most effective on the battlefield were the French Zouaves, picturesque in their turbans, blue waistcoats, and red puffed trousers. They attacked without even waiting for orders, going forward at their *pas de charge*, 'leaping like kangaroos'. The French were too much for the Russians. At this new onset they began to withdraw from the field.

The British were too exhausted to harass and pursue their retreating foe, and the French commander-in-chief proved strangely unwilling to do so, though he was given a splendid chance to ram his victory home. General Canrobert, always the political general, was beginning to become enmeshed in a military intrigue, extending from Paris to the Crimea itself, which for far too long was to bog the fighting down, even after the mud of Balaclava had dried out, and the long, hard winter had given place to spring.

After the Battle of Inkerman, the dead lay so thick on the field that a horseman could not ride across it, even picking his way. The Russians lost no less than 12,000 men, mostly dead on the field. Their losses may have been as high as 20,000. British casualties were 632 dead (of whom 43 were officers) and 1,873 wounded. French casualties, killed and wounded, amounted to 1,726. Of the total Russian army of 100,000, only a part, between 20,000 and 30,000, had successfully been deployed on to the field of battle. The impetus of this immense force had been held, at the height of the action, by less than 4,000 British soldiers, fighting with no battle plan to speak of, and almost no ammunition.

Inkerman was, in fact, the turning point in the war. The Russians, though this time coming down on their weakened foe in vast numbers, had for a second time failed to cut the

British off from Balaclava Bay, or drive them into the sea – and war seldom gives third chances. Sebastopol, therefore, was bound, in the end, to fall – no fortress, however badly invested however brilliantly defended, can hold out forever.

Disorganized though their administration might be, so long as the allies kept command of the sea, they would continue to be supplied. Faults in organization and leadership could, in time, be put right, supplies built up, and an effective fighting general found, at last, to plan and lead the final assault.

The Russians, by contrast, rigid inside their imperial dictatorship, with an army of dimly-comprehending peasants, and a state based on censorship and police terror, could not take the strain of continual defeat. The Russian political structure was based on faith and unthinking obedience. Doubts and questionings would begin to make it crack.

The British could, in fact, replace during 1855 everything they had lost in 1854 – except the men who had won their victories, their splendid professional army, trained over many years on the barrack square, and destroyed by disease and incompetence in one winter.

The government in London was soon to announce plans for hiring continental troops, and recruiting a foreign legion. But mercenaries, however well paid, could never be relied upon to fight so magnificently as had the hungry and disease-ridden British infantrymen on the day of Inkerman.

7

The Lady with the Lamp

'GOOD God!' exclaimed Dr Alexander, a staff surgeon, as he
went ashore with the Light Division at Calamita Bay. 'They
have landed this army without any kind of hospital transport!'

The reality was even grimmer, as the Battle of Alma was
soon to show. There were no bandages and no splints, no
morphine and no chloroform. As the soft lead balls fired
from Russian muskets mushroomed against a living target,
they smashed up arm and leg bones hideously, so that ampu-
tations were frequent – and had to be carried out after the
battle with no anaesthetic, often by moonlight.

The wounded, mingled with the sick, were then carried by
soldiers down to the boats on the shore, unless they were
lucky enough to find a place in an araba – a jolting native
cart without springs. The turbulent voyage across the Black
Sea to the British hospital at Scutari, opposite Constantinople, sometimes took fourteen days. The wounded
were left to lie on the deck planks in the bloodstained clothes
they had been wearing when they were carried from the
field. Their food was salt pork and ship's biscuit. Those sick
of cholera lay cheek by jowl with those suffering from
wounds. In voyages that winter from Balaclava to the Bosphorus, the average death rate at sea was ten per cent.

Few of the army surgeons dared be as outspoken as Dr
Alexander. A medical doctor's job in civil life would, for
most of them, have been difficult to find and keep. Army
surgeons, in those days, need not be well qualified or highly
competent. During the long years of peace they had learned
the importance of keeping their paperwork in good order,

and their tone of voice, when addressing senior officers, respectful.

Dr John Hall, head of army medical services in the theatre of war, and a man much feared by his subordinates, actually opposed the use of chloroform in surgical operations. There was none to be had in the Crimea, anyway; but that, in his opinion, was all to the good, since, 'the smart shock of the knife was a powerful stimulant'.

On 20 October, after sensational reports from W. H. Russell to *The Times* about the treatment of wounded men had begun to stir up anger and protest in Britain, Dr John Hall reported to Lord Raglan that the British hospitals in Scutari were in a 'highly satisfactory state'. This, as he knew from long years of experience, was exactly the sort of report that harassed superiors liked to get from their medical staff. The report happened not to be true, but Lord Raglan was not likely to go and see for himself.

A soldier entering a hospital was assumed to have brought his knapsack with him, and his blanket. He would draw all his personal necessities in the hospital from his own pack. But the sick coming from Calamita Bay, like the wounded at Alma, had discarded their packs on the order of their officers. When they arrived in the hospital, they had, therefore, no clean change of clothes, no soap or towel. Most of them had nothing better to cover themselves with than a bloodstained greatcoat.

Now army regulations on the issue of all supplies, even to hospitals, had on purpose been made complicated and difficult, to save money in peacetime. This was why the wounded, when they reached the hospital in Scutari, were obliged to lie in filth – because there was almost no way the hospital staff could supply them with soap and clean linen, unless someone was courageous enough to break the rules and regulations. And who would jeopardize his career by doing that?

But could not the ward orderlies at least have washed the

(*Top*) The Grenadier Guards leave Trafalgar Square on 22 February 1854 for the Crimea (Mary Evans Picture Library)

(*Above*) The harbour at Balaclava (The Queen's Collection)

(*Top*) Lord Palmerston
(National Portrait Gallery)
(*Above*) William Russell
(*The Times*)

(*Top*) Florence Nightingale
(The Queen's Collection)
(*Above*) Omar Pasha
(The Queen's Collection)

(*Top*) The Highlanders attacking the Russian redoubt at the
Battle of Alma (The Mansell Collection)

(*Above*) The Russian retreat from the south side of Sebastopol
(The Mansell Collection)

(*Top*) Coldstream Guards
(The Queen's Collection)

(*Above*) The 47th Foot in
winter (Photo by courtesy of the
Gernsheim Collection)

(*Top*) The Royal Navy
(The Queen's Collection)

(*Above*) Seaman on his way to
Balaclava, by camel (The
Queen's Collection)

[By John Leech.]

"GENERAL FÉVRIER" TURNED TRAITOR.

"RUSSIA HAS TWO GENERALS IN WHOM SHE CAN CONFIDE—GENERALS JANVIER AND FÉVRIER."—*Speech of the late Emperor of Russia.*

[February 10, 1855.—Vol. 28, p. 55.]

(*Top*) General February proved no friend to the Russians, as this *Punch* cartoon of 1855 shows (Mary Evans Picture Library)

(*Left*) What you needed as a soldier in the Crimea (Mary Evans Picture Library)

(*Top*) Lord Raglan
(National Portrait Gallery)

(*Above*) Lord Lucan
(National Army Museum)

(*Top*) Lord Cardigan

(*Above*) Captain Lewis Nolan
(*Illustrated London News*)

(*Top*) The Charge of the
Light Brigade at Balaclava
(The Mansell Collection)

(*Above*) Storming the
Malakoff (The Queen's
Collection)

(*Left*) The interior of the
Malakoff (The Queen's
Collection)

(*Top*) Florence
Nightingale in the
hospital at Scutari
(*Illustrated London
News*)

(*Left*) Crimean Wa[r]
casualties (The
Queen's Collection

(*Below*) Queen
Victoria inspects th[e]
Crimean wounded
(Mary Evans Pictu[re]
Library)

men, as they arrived from their ordeal on board ship?

This, too, was asking too much. In the British army there were no regular medical orderlies, trained for their work, as with the French. In the two enormous British army hospitals at Scutari – hospitals in name only, one had formerly been the barracks of the Turkish Artillery – there were a dozen worn-out veterans, some of them drunkards or men dodging frontline duty.

Even had they been willing to work – and most of them were more interested in stealing the rations of men too weak to know they were being robbed – the sick and wounded came in too fast. Even devoted and willing hands, as the battles occurred and the cholera spread, would have made little impression on the heap of human suffering that covered the floors and lined the endless corridors.

Once again, in October 1854, the British taxpayer, as he propped *The Times* against the marmalade pot on his breakfast table, was obliged to start his day by reading such gloomy and infuriating dispatches as this:

Not only are there not sufficient surgeons . . . not only are there no dressers or nurses . . . there is not even linen to make bandages. There is no preparation for the commonest surgical operations. Not only are the men kept, in some cases, for a week, without the hand of a medical man coming near their wounds, not only are they left to expire in agony . . . it is found that the commonest appliances of a workhouse sick ward are wanting, and that the men must die through the medical staff of the British Army having forgotten that old rags are necessary for the dressing of wounds.

And these neglected men were the heroes of the heights of Alma!

The answer of the army authorities was that such reports helped the enemy, and must be repressed. But for once, this customary answer was not effective; the uproar grew.

As the outcry became nationwide, large sums of money were collected, to buy relief supplies. Immediate changes were demanded. But the British army had been run like this as long as anyone could remember – and armies have ingenious ways of making things awkward for civilian reformers. To transform the hell that was Scutari required a miracle. And where on earth would the British government find someone who could work miracles?

To be young, beautiful, rich, intelligent, and witty – to move in the highest society and be courted by some of the most fascinating men of the day – all this, surely, should have been enough to fill a young girl's life.

But Florence Nightingale had a secret passion. What it was, none of the fashionable young men who danced with her at the ball or observed and admired her appearance in her box at the opera was ever allowed to find out. This secret passion – this obsession – was bitterly opposed by her family, most of all by her mother. Florence, after a night at the ball, would get up at the crack of dawn to read books on the subject of her obsession, and make elaborate notes. Whenever she could slip away from her mother's watchfulness, and indulge her secret desire, she would do so.

Her passion was for nursing. It was driving her family to despair.

When, at the end of the season, the Nightingales left fashionable London and returned to their country estate, Florence would go off to the cottages of the poor, to wash and tend sick old women. She had refused several handsome offers of marriage. Despite her beauty and wit and popularity, she would soon be at the age when any Victorian girl must resign herself to being a spinster. 'I can do without marriage or intellect or social intercourse, or anything of the things people sigh after,' she wrote. 'Nursing satisfies my soul . . . I want nothing else, I am at home. My heart is filled.'

If a girl revealed such a passion for nursing nowadays, most parents would be happy to let her satisfy it. Nursing is a respected profession, demanding self-sacrifice, and does honour to the girls who choose it. But then it was different.

Nurses in the mid-nineteenth century were of two sorts.

Some, usually in Catholic countries, were members of religious orders – nuns vowed to a lifetime of service. They were often women of noble character, but as nurses, were sometimes not very effective or scientific. In Protestant England, however, nurses were usually drunken and immoral, often dirty, and generally lacking in professional training. Though there might be exceptions, they were rare.

Nursing, therefore, was a job for a woman reckless of her reputation. When Florence Nightingale first confessed to her family that she wished to go into a hospital and study nursing, her parents took it for granted that she must be 'in love with some low, vulgar surgeon'. In those days, no respectable young woman ever went into a hospital to serve the sick.

Florence Nightingale, however, was descended, on both sides of her family, from people in the habit of doing exactly what they chose. Her paternal grandfather was the notorious Mad Peter Nightingale, an eccentric Derbyshire squire who had been a daredevil steeplechaser and hard drinker. Her great-grandfather on her mother's side, a British merchant, had once owned considerable property in North America, but had given it up voluntarily during the Revolutionary War to show his sympathy with the Americans who followed George Washington.

This man's son, Florence Nightingale's grandfather, was for forty-six years an abolitionist Member of Parliament. He not only fought slavery, but also defended factory workers, Dissenters and Jews at a time in Britain when to speak out in public for such despised minorities was unpopular.

When she was twenty-four, Florence Nightingale sought advice from an American friend then in England, Julia Ward Howe, who was to become famous for writing 'The Battle Hymn of the Republic'. Florence asked, 'Do you think it would be unsuitable and unbecoming for a young Englishwoman to devote herself to works of charity in hospitals? . . . Do you think it would be a dreadful thing?' To this earnest question, Julia Ward Howe wisely answered, 'My dear, it would be unusual, and in England, whatever is unusual is thought to be unsuitable, but I say to you "go forward" if you have a vocation for that way of life, act up to your inspiration.'

In 1851, when she was thirty-one, and her parents began to realize that she would never marry, Florence managed, at last, to persuade her family to let her go on a visit to a Protestant hospital in Germany. This hospital was run entirely by women – no male surgeon was in attendance, and even the apothecary was a woman, so what harm could it do her reputation?

Then, in August of 1853, came a chance to run a hospital for the Distressed Gentlewomen's Association – a charity for governesses, run by titled ladies. Here, Miss Nightingale began to show herself a clever and thrifty administrator, as well as a devoted nurse. To the delight of the aristocratic board of management, she reduced the daily expenditure on patients from 1s 9d to 1s and yet the standard of nursing had improved. (The patients were not badly fed, either. In those days a shilling bought very much more than it does today.)

In the summer of 1854, when the new wave of cholera moving around the world reached Britain, there was a serious outbreak in London. Florence Nightingale volunteered to work among cholera victims in the Middlesex Hospital, and found herself there among the poorest and most wretched women from the streets of London. In such a grave emergency, the prejudice against her working in hospitals vanished.

Florence Nightingale was tall, very slight, with thick, rich brown hair, which she wore rather short. Her eyes were grey and cool. Men and women alike came under her spell, and found themselves bent to her iron will. Her mother, realizing at last that all opposition to nursing was useless, exclaimed, 'We are ducks who have hatched a wild swan.'

Sidney Herbert, Secretary at War, was one of the men who had come under the influence of Florence Nightingale's powerful personality. Indeed, he was secretly in love with her. Though in office he had done his best to fight the abuses and absurdities of the army system, eventually he himself became a victim, and he was forced to resign to appease the anger of political critics. How, indeed, was the hospital system at Scutari to be changed in time to save men's lives when control was split among three departments of state, with every official involved in decisions an expert in passing the buck? Who could work the necessary miracle?

The Times went on thundering and threatening. In Parliament, searching questions were being asked. A fund of £30,000 had by now been collected to relieve the sick and wounded. To satisfy the roar of public opinion, why not send out Miss Nightingale, with a band of nurses?

'The French,' W. H. Russell had pointed out in a recent dispatch, 'are greatly our superiors. Their medical arrangements are extremely good, their surgeons are more numerous, and they also have the help of the Sisters of Charity ... these devoted women are excellent nurses.' Next day, a letter in *The Times* demanded, '*Why have we no Sisters of Charity?*' Miss Nightingale might be the next best thing.

All London was scoured for nurses. Though Florence Nightingale had been asked to take out forty, only twenty even fairly reliable professional nurses could be found. For most of them, she admitted, 'money was the only inducement – the "enthusiasm" of the nursing in the Crimean campaign, that is all bosh.' Miss Nightingale recruited her nurses by offering them nearly double the money they could earn in London – with steeply rising increases of pay on condition of good behaviour. A nurse invalided home was to go first class. A nurse guilty of misconduct – drunkenness, or fraternizing with the troops – would be sent home third class, on salt rations. Nurses were to be allowed out of the hospital only in parties of four, and never without leave.

To make up her number, Florence Nightingale also took with her a group of Roman Catholic and Anglican nuns, some of whom had recent experience in nursing cholera. However, as Sisters of Mercy these nuns were not always effective. 'More fit for heaven than a hospital,' said Florence later, 'they flit about like angels without hands, among the patients, and soothe their souls, while they leave their bodies dirty and neglected.'

All her nurses were dressed in a uniform that was deliberately ugly – a grey tweed dress, grey worsted jacket, plain white cap, and short woollen cloak. Over their shoulders, on a holland scarf, were embroidered in red the words, *Scutari Hospital.*

Sidney Herbert had assured Florence Nightingale that she would find all necessary medical stores at Scutari, in abundance. He was judging by the official reports that had been sent to his office. Indeed, anyone who read simply the official reports would believe there was nothing whatever wrong at Scutari. Even Florence herself, before she left London, began to wonder if the newspaper reports might not be exaggerated. But she took out a quantity of useful stores with her, just in case.

As their ship approached Constantinople, one of the Anglican nuns said, 'Ah, Miss Nightingale, when we land, let us go straight to nursing the poor fellows.' 'The strongest,' answered Florence Nightingale curtly, 'will be wanted at the wash-tub.'

The Battle of Balaclava had been fought on 25 October, and the wounded were already on their way across the Black Sea. As the newly arrived nurses were rowed in a caïque from Seraglio Point, in Constantinople, across to the Scutari side, they found the sea near the Barrack Hospital filthy with refuse. On shore, stray dogs were tearing at the carcass of a dead horse. Coming closer to the hospital, they could smell the foul odour of decay and death long before they entered its doors.

Inside the Barrack Hospital there were four miles of occupied beds, crammed side by side. The courtyard outside was a swamp of filth. The walls inside were streaming with dampness. In the basement lingered two hundred soldiers' wives, abandoned, cholera-ridden, neglecting their children, drowning their sorrows in drink. The physical condition of the thousands of sick and wounded men was disgusting beyond belief. Fever, cholera, gangrene, and lice tormented them. They were all unbelievably dirty.

During the first three weeks of their stay in the hospital – weeks during which the army medical authorities went on using every dodge to ignore the nurses and prevent their being employed – Florence Nightingale observed no body linen being washed, and saw no basin, towel, or soap in any of the wards.

The men's rations were of boiled meat, cooked in thirteen large copper cauldrons. Sometimes the sick man was unlucky, and got not meat but bone. Anyway, to cholera patients, the eating of meat was a physical agony. Immediately after, without being washed or rinsed, the same copper cauldrons were used for boiling tea.

The senior medical officers were obliged to spend most of their time filling up official forms. Some of the army surgeons, Florence found, were devoted to their profession, and anxious always to do their best; but, in the face of such a mountain of problems, they, too, were in despair. 'Their heads,' wrote Florence Nightingale, 'are so flattened between the boards of army discipline that they remain old children all their lives.'

Wisely, patiently, Miss Nightingale hardened her heart and bided her time. The hospital authorities had made it very clear that they did not want her, and would like to find some way of getting rid of her. They knew perfectly well that once a woman of her high political and social connections had seen for herself what the hospital was like, the ugly truth about Scutari could no longer be concealed or denied. And, when the scandal was investigated officially, someone – indeed, any one of them – might find himself the scapegoat for the faults inherent in the system.

All sorts of tactics were tried. The desperately over-crowded apartment they gave the nurses to sleep in was found to contain the corpse of a deceased Russian general.

During those first few weeks the nurses, though growing restive against Florence Nightingale's firm discipline, were kept busy tearing up linen and rolling bandages and scrubbing out their quarters. Their time would come.

Could high official pressure perhaps be brought to bear? The most influential man in Constantinople was the British Ambassador, Viscount Stratford de Redcliffe, who had been here in the diplomatic service, on and off, since 1808, and wielded enormous influence with the Turks. In Constantinople, he could achieve almost anything he wanted.

His instructions from London were to cooperate fully with Miss Nightingale. But since Dr Menzies, the senior medical officer, had told him in a report that nothing whatever was lacking at Scutari, Sir Stratford ignored what *The Times* had to say, and never went to look at the British hospitals for himself. Florence Nightingale described him as 'bad-hearted, heartless, pompous and lazy', and she can hardly be blamed for her harsh opinion. Since it had been proved officially that all was well at Scutari, he suggested to her that the money collected in Britain to buy medical comforts might be better spent on building a Protestant Church in Constantinople.

Some of the army officers, Miss Nightingale found, had a no less heartless attitude towards the common soldiers. They described their men as 'animals ... blackguards ... scum', and told her, 'You will spoil the brutes.' Clean bedding, hospital clothing, soup were, in their eyes, 'preposterous luxuries'.

On Sunday, 5 November, however, when the wounded from the Battle of Balaclava started to arrive, Miss Nightingale and her nurses could be frozen out no longer. Unless every willing pair of hands went to work at once, the hospital would be utterly overwhelmed. Florence Nightingale's great chance had come.

Driven by overwhelming pressure to ask the nurses for their help, the army surgeons watched them carefully, even so, to see if they were reliable. And they were. The senior medical officer admitted that the most experienced of the nurses, Mrs Roberts, 'dressed wounds or fractures better than any of the dressers or assistant surgeons'. He went on to explain that his misgivings about employing nurses, except in an emergency like this, were 'not a question of efficiency, nor of the comfort of the patients, but of the regulations of the service'. The regulations were sacred.

Just how a mean-minded man could turn the 'regulations of the service' to his own advantage was soon to be shown when Florence Nightingale did some invalid cookery of her own. The cholera patients were finding boiled meat (or the water it had been boiled in, if on a 'spoon diet') horribly painful to digest. The regulations, however, said that no nurse could give a patient nourishment, except when a doctor directed. The nurses, seeing men dying under their eyes for want of food, started to rebel, so Florence Nightingale started cooking them dishes of the invalid food she had brought out from England.

This deliberate breach of the regulations caused resentment in the Purveyor. It was his job to give out food and supplies bought by the Commissariat, though, since he had only one clerk to issue rations to 2,500 patients, some of the sick and wounded men were likely to go hungry. But, as his lifetime of experience told him, so long as he kept to the letter of the regulations, he was safe.

An unexpected visit was paid to the hospital by the Duke of Cambridge, the royal prince who had commanded the Guards so bravely at Alma and Inkerman. (This visit was most exceptional. Dr Brush of the Scots Greys, who ran a hospital in the Crimea itself, later told a commission of inquiry, 'During the time I have been in the Crimea . . . no general officer has visited my hospital, nor, to my knowledge, in any way interested himself about the sick.') The Duke told Dr Menzies how extremely dissatisfied he was with the dinners given men from his brigade. This gave the Purveyor the opening he needed.

When Dr Menzies passed on the Duke's complaint, the

Purveyor informed him that the men's dinners were bad simply and solely because Miss Nightingale had lately been occupying the kitchens, to cook her invalid food. But Florence Nightingale had, in fact, been too clever for him. She had taken the precaution always of cooking her dishes of soup and arrowroot in the nurses' quarters on their own stove. The Purveyor's glib and damaging lie, therefore, did her no harm – but it was at this unheroic level of petty slander that Florence Nightingale was obliged to begin her fight to save the soldiers' lives.

The system of providing necessaries for the wounded was unbelievably elaborate. The Commissariat delivered standard rations and the fuel to cook them, but not invalid food. The Purveyor was expected to supply what were known as 'medical comforts' – including invalid food. He did not, however, buy them – the Commissariat did that. Since the Purveyor never dealt directly with the merchants, he could never complain effectively about poor quality.

Any doctor might order a man to be put on an invalid diet. But whether the man actually got his special food depended on the Purveyor. Both Commissariat and Purveyor were allowed, by the regulations, to supply only certain named articles, and no others. Any medical officer giving a man invalid food not on the list was 'personally and financially responsible to the Government', that is, he would eventually have to pay for the article out of his own pocket. One simple instance will show how this might work in practice. Lime juice was used by the British navy in those days to fight against scurvy. Twenty thousand pounds weight of lime juice arrived in Constantinople on 10 December, for the use of the army. None was issued until February – though in every ward at Scutari men were dying of scurvy – because no order existed for the inclusion of lime juice on the daily ration. In such a crazy jungle of treacherous regulations, it took moral courage not to shut one's ears to the groans of the sufferers, and simply do nothing.

After Inkerman, however, sick and wounded men began

to pour into the Barrack Hospital without warning. All opposition to Miss Nightingale and her nurses gave way. She had been spending money from charity, and from her own purse, to build up a stock of hospital necessaries in defiance of the regulations. She had been shrewdly testing the men on whom she might rely. Now she began to work her miracle.

In the small room where she sat at a plain wooden table, writing requests, orders, letters, reports, there was a narrow bed – but she seldom slept. She not only did a huge amount of administrative work, but also spent hours in the wards, nursing. She had her personal attendant, Robert Robinson, an invalided eleven-year-old drummer boy from the 68th Light Infantry, who ran messages, and at night carried her lamp, while she went among the crowds of wounded to help during an operation, or sat by a man in the moment of death.

The sheer volume of paper work after Balaclava and Inkerman had finally left the Purveyor's Department paralysed and helpless. Their complicated system was never meant for the realities of war. Florence Nightingale took over this job entirely, and this time bought not 'what the regulations allowed', but all that was really needed – simple but vital necessities, like two hundred scrubbing brushes.

In her thin, angular, neat writing she wrote, late at night, to Sidney Herbert, 'We are lucky in our medical heads – two of them are brutes, and four are angels – for this is a work which makes angels or devils of men.' Everything, at Scutari, had now to be done again, from the start.

For the past five weeks, no clothes at all had been washed, though new arrivals, as they came off the boats, were so filthy that they would cry out to the nurses, 'Don't touch us!' Florence Nightingale got a boiler – and set the soldiers' wives, despairingly encamped in the hospital basement, to the work of washing clothes. The everyday filth of the hospital was beyond belief. As the chaplain knelt, paper in hand, to take the last message of a dying man, he found that before he could write one word, the paper in his hand would be speckled with lice.

This chaplain, the Reverend Sidney Godolphin Osborne, a staunch supporter of Florence Nightingale, very soon found that he was taking an active part in surgical operations. Augustus Stafford, a Member of Parliament who had travelled out to Scutari to see for himself, had a saucepan thrust into his hand on arrival, and found himself feeding the sick. It was small details that made all the difference – the screens Miss Nightingale bought, so men could be operated on without their comrades being forced to watch; the massive cleaning of the lavatories, when it was found that, though 1,000 men were ill with acute diarrhoea, the entire hospital possessed only 20 chamber pots; the 6,000 shirts, bought with her own money, so that men, at last, could sleep in something clean.

At the beginning of December, though fighting had practically ceased, Lord Raglan reported to Scutari that 500 sick men were on their way. There was simply nowhere to put them. The death rate in the hospital was incredibily high, yet the dead were not making room for the living fast enough to fit in 500 more victims of life in the winter trenches.

One tower of the barracks had been burned out in a fire. Florence Nightingale paid the wages of 200 Turkish workmen to repair and equip it at top speed – and got the job finished in time. When the sick men arrived, still haunted by their hellish memories of the Crimea, one of them said, 'We felt we were in heaven.'

Between 17 December and 3 January, 4,000 men arrived at the two Scutari hospitals, as the British army before Sebastopol slowly destroyed itself. By 8 January the hospitals held 12,000 men. One deadly circumstance puzzled all of them: though the Scutari hospitals were organized at last, and the men were better fed and properly nursed, yet still the death rate rose. Men who came in wounded were catching the diseases of those who came in sick. Those who came in with scurvy were catching cholera. Even medical officers began to fear entering the wards.

Florence Nightingale herself fearlessly continued her rounds each night. She would pause by the bedside of one dying man and then another, to comfort his last moments by the light of the lamp carried by the drummer boy. Wounded men were observed to turn and kiss the shadow thrown by her lamp on the wall as she passed. Later, of the common soldiers in Scutari, she declared, 'Never came from any one of them one word nor one look which a gentleman would not have used ... there arose above it all the innate dignity, gentleness and chivalry of the men ... shining in the midst of what must be considered the lowest sinks of human misery.'

Yet, still the death rate rose. In three months, 9,000 good soldiers had died in the Barrack Hospital alone. It was later estimated that three quarters of all the casualties suffered by the British army in the Crimean War had been from diseases caught in the hospital – diseases such as dysentery, typhoid, and cholera. By January 1855 the Brigade of Guards was reduced to 300 men, the Scots Fusiliers to 78, and the 63rd Regiment had disappeared entirely.

The hospital itself seemed to be killing the men who came within its own four walls.

Florence Nightingale's descriptions of life and death at Scutari were beginning to be read in London by many influential people, beginning with the Queen, and including Lord Palmerston, the new Prime Minister. Plans were on foot to reform army medical services along the lines Miss Nightingale recommended. At the end of February, sent out post-haste to solve the mystery of those endless deaths in Scutari's hospitals, came the Sanitary Commission – practical engineers with a knowledge of modern sanitation, and the power to act. As Miss Nightingale said afterwards, they 'saved the British Army'.

Their first inspection produced a one-word condemnation of this hospital that formerly had been a Turkish barracks: *murderous*. Its foundations stood in a sea of decaying filth. The water supply was permanently contaminated – drinking water reached the hospital through the decaying carcass of a horse. The Sanitary Commission began at once to flush the sewers, lime-wash the walls, get rid of the rats. The mortality dropped magically, from 14½ per cent in the week ending 7 April, to 5·2 per cent in the week ending 19 May.

Helping Miss Nightingale had now become fashionable. In March 1855, out from London came M. Alexis Soyer, chef at the Reform Club. With his small, pointed beard and extravagant manner, he looked like a Frenchman in a comic opera. Yet M. Soyer had high government backing, and really knew his job. He had studied how to cook large quantities of food economically, and yet serve delicious dishes. Rapidly, he transformed the hospital kitchens, then he invited the British Ambassador and Lady Stratford de Redcliffe to visit the hospital (at last!), where he fed them an excellent meal, made strictly with army rations. He invented a special cooking oven, the Soyer boiler, used long after, and the 'Scutari teapot', which would make tea for half a company of men. When M. Soyer returned to the Reform Club he left behind him fifty men who had become expert cooks, trained in his methods.

The crisis was over. By May 1855 all was very different. Two hundred sick men, arriving on the *Severn*, were properly received and washed; their hair was cut. They were given clean hospital gowns, put into decent beds, and given good food. As one soldier was overheard to say, 'If Florence Nightingale were at our head, we would take Sebastopol next week.'

Florence Nightingale 'never let any man who was under her observation die alone'. She had, that winter, sat at two thousand deathbeds. 'Before she came, there was cursing and swearing,' said one soldier. 'But, after that, it was holy as a church.'

'The real humiliation,' she had written to Sidney Herbert, in the black days, 'the real hardship of this place, is that we have to do with men who are neither gentlemen, nor men of education, nor even men of business, nor men of feeling, but men whose only object is to keep themselves out of blame.' But a handful of men in the army medical services with moral courage had come under her eye, and were already on the ladder of promotion.

Florence Nightingale's personal motive in coming to the Crimea had been, at first, to prove that women from good homes could be trusted as nurses – to help establish nursing as a new and honoured profession for women. In this, she had succeeded. Now, her health undermined by a winter in which she had endured labour and danger to a degree almost super-human, Florence Nightingale gave herself a new task – of making sure that never again would a British army go into action without efficient medical services.

'I stand,' she said, 'at the altar of the murdered men, and while I live, I will fight their cause.'

8

Inside Sebastopol

A LONG way forward from the bastions of Sebastopol,
Colonel Todleben had sent sharpshooters into foxholes
screened with a few sandbags, or a pile of stones, to snipe at
men working in the French or British lines. Later, he would
try to connect these foxholes by trenches, and they had again
and again to be cleared at the point of the bayonet by allied
squads moving dangerously across the open.

Sooner or later, however, as Todleben knew, the allied
trenches would come close enough to the outer fortifications
of Sebastopol for allied infantry to rush forth from them and
risk an assault – after the heavy siege guns had silenced the
Russian artillery, and battered the walls of the redoubts.

Once inside the city, though the attackers might have to
fight street by street, they were bound to take Sebastopol in
the end. In military strategy, a fortress was simply an elaborate delaying device, which gave a field army time to mobilize
for battle. Sooner or later, however cleverly and bravely it
might be defended, a fortress, if scientifically assaulted, was
bound to fall.

The only question now was – when?

The British Cabinet, after the victory at Alma, had been
so sure the fall of Sebastopol would be quick – certainly
before the onset of winter – that there was actually no Cabinet meeting between the months of August and October
1854. The bloody contests at Balaclava and Inkerman had
proved that the British could not be pushed into the sea. But
how long would it take them and their French allies to break
through Colonel Todleben's intricate defences?

Through the hideous winter months, Allies and Russians

slowly approached each other. No-man's-land shrank, and the trenches crept closer. Opposite Flagstaff Bastion, working up to their knees in liquid mud, the French had arrived within 180 yards of the enemy. The British, on the thin, stony soil of Mount Inkerman, had slowly begun digging a second parallel. Only a handful of them were fit to work.

Indeed, had the Russians but known, there was one day, in January 1855, when the British could muster a total of only 290 fit men in their left and right attacks, and on Mount Inkerman – this was when nearly 6,000 Russian soldiers manned the enemy positions opposite. The odds that day were twenty to one against the British, but the reputation for ferocity they had gained at Inkerman stood them then, and later, in good stead. In fact, throughout the campaign, and later, even in their official histories, the Russian High Command wildly exaggerated the numbers of the allied enemy. They could never bring themselves to admit that only the thin red line had held them back.

After Inkerman, the Russians took thousands of men from their field army into Sebastopol, and set them to work on the defences. Colonel Todleben proceeded to extend the trenches that connected his foxholes, thereby advancing his line. This obliged the outnumbered and harassed British to dig their own forward foxhole system, and make the Russians keep their heads down, by sniping. On 20 November, British riflemen managed to drive the Russians out of their forward line of pits, with cold steel. On 24 March, ready for the spring campaign, at the heavy cost of 1,300 killed and wounded, the Russians, in a strong sortie, managed to drive French and British for a while out of their advanced trenches, and to establish a new line of rifle pits within eighty yards of the French line. It was a grim sort of winter warfare.

In the soil near the French lines, which was deep, the war of mine and countermine also continued. This was a game at which the French excelled. The underground gallery they were driving towards Flagstaff Bastion was detected by the

Russians, who kept a listening watch for the sound of pick-axes striking home. The Russians managed to dig a counter-mine under the French mine, and blow it into the winter air.

Before Flagstaff Bastion was a smooth, sloping glacis – a bare approach where the French, when it came to the moment of attack, must break from cover and risk being shot down. The French decided they would break up this glacis, and give themselves shelter amid the rubble. They placed a mine of gunpowder in a gallery that ran just short of the bastion, and blew it. But the Russians at once sallied out to occupy the crater – yet again extending their lines.

All winter through, the Russians, on balance, showed more dash, rapidity, and audacity than the allies. They were lucky to have, in Colonel Todleben, a scientific soldier with a touch of genius. The Allies were led by Lord Raglan, an elderly English gentleman whose many fine qualities of mind and character did not include several of those essential to generalship; and François Canrobert, whose devious nature had been formed in the schools of colonial warfare, political controversy, and the shooting down of unarmed civilians.

One of the Russian officers taken from the field army after the defeat at Inkerman, and sent into Sebastopol, was a second-lieutenant of artillery called Count Leo Tolstoy. At twenty-six, Tolstoy was old for a second lieutenant. Promotion had come slowly to him. Even a medal promised him when fighting the Turks in the Caucasus had failed to arrive, and the reason was typically Russian. Somewhere or other his papers had been lost. Without them, he could expect neither medals nor promotion.

As seen by his comrades-in-arms, Count Tolstoy was a wild and witty young man, a desperate card player, well connected but often in debt. He was related to General Gorchakov, who had succeeded Menshikov as commander-in-chief for the Russians. Tolstoy was acknowledged to be a man almost recklessly brave. If he was also given to reading

French novels and scribbling quietly in a notebook – well, every man is entitled to his little personal peculiarities.

When he was in the Caucasus, Tolstoy had written an autobiography, called *Childhood*, which was soon to bring him great celebrity, and the account he was writing in his notebook now about the fighting in Sebastopol was to bring him even greater fame. To his comrades, Leo Tolstoy was known merely as a brave and even reckless gunner subaltern, but in a few years he would be recognized as one of the greatest writers in the Russian language.

After the defeat at Inkerman, Leo Tolstoy wrote fervently in his diary:

We had to retreat, because half our army had no cannon, because of impassable roads, terrible slaughter. These men, who are now offering their lives, will be Russia's citizens, and will not forget their sacrifice. The enthusiasm aroused in them by the war will stamp self-sacrifice and nobleness for ever on their character.

In this exalted frame of mind, he took up his new duties in the fortress city, joining the 2nd Battery of the Light Artillery Brigade in the town itself. 'Having seen all our fortifications,' he wrote, 'to take Sebastopol is quite impossible.'

A fortnight's stay in the besieged city began to alter his tone of voice. By 5 November 1854 he was writing, 'I left Sebastopol for the front, more convinced than before that Russia must fall, or completely reorganize herself.'

He had, not long before, spent some time chatting with wounded British and French soldiers, held prisoner. He observed:

Each of them is proud of his position, and respects himself. Good weapons and the skill to use them, youth, and some idea of politics, make them conscious of their own dignity. With us, stupid drill for dressing the file and saluting with the musket, useless weapons, ignorance, and bad food, destroy the men's interest, their last spark of pride, and give them even too high an opinion of the enemy.

'When Kornilov rode through the troops,' Leo Tolstoy

noted, 'instead of the usual salute, he said, "*You will have to die, boys – die!*" And the troops yelled back, "*We will die, your Excellency – hurrah!*" Twenty-two thousand have kept their word.' He wrote, with bitter personal knowledge, of his kinsman, General Gorchakov, as someone typical of 'generals who have lost their senses, their feeling, and their enterprise'.

Yet, remembering Sebastopol itself, Tolstoy expressed an almost reckless determination to die in the city's defence – a mood he shared with his comrades-in-arms. To his brother Sergius, Second-Lieutenant Tolstoy proudly wrote:

We have more than 500 guns, and several lines of heavy earthworks. I spent a week in that fortress, and to my last day used to lose my way amid the labyrinth of batteries, as in a wood. A company of Marines nearly mutinied, because they were to be withdrawn from batteries in which they had been exposed to shellfire for 30 days. The priests with their crosses go to the bastions and read prayers under fire. In one brigade, the 24th, more than 160 wounded men would not leave the front. Do not forget that we, with equal or inferior forces, and armed only with bayonets, and with the worst troops in the Russian Army (such as the 6th Corps), are fighting a more numerous enemy, aided by a fleet, armed with 3,000 cannon, excellently supplied with rifles. I do not even mention the superiority of their generals.

The vividness, the patriotic fervour of Tolstoy's first account of the siege, 'Sebastopol in December', when published in St Petersburg, created a sensation. The Dowager Empress wept as she read it. The new Tsar, Alexander, reputedly more liberal-minded than dead Nicholas, gave secret orders to 'take care of the life of that young man'.

Tolstoy, however, was angry with the censor, who not only cut out certain passages, but had impertinently added a few super-patriotic touches of his own. Now he was to be annoyed still further, by being sent to join a mountain battery up-country, where his life would be 'taken care of', but his chance of seeing action was remote.

The second tour of duty Tolstoy managed to wangle in

Sebastopol was from 1 April 1855 to 15 May, when spring weather had come and the massive bombardments started up again – when the British and French armies, heavily reinforced, were beginning to apply the pressure.

Attended by his serf Alexis – given him as a present when he entered the University, and now occupied with the risky job of bringing his master's rations to the front – Count Leo Tolstoy went to join a battery in what the Russians called the Fourth Bastion. The Allies had nicknamed it the Flagstaff Bastion – the exposed redoubt that came closest to the French lines. In intervals of his strenuous duty there, Tolstoy wrote a narrative of life in the bastion, and at the same time made entries like these in his diary:

There has been bombardment and nothing else for six days, and this is my fourth day in Sebastopol. We are short of powder. Our losses already amount to 5,000, but we are holding out. Wrote two pages of 'Sebastopol' in the evening. What a fine spirit there is among the sailors! My little soldiers are also nice, and I am cheerful when with them. Yesterday, a fifth mine exploded. Today, have finished 'Sebastopol'. The constant charm of danger is so pleasant that I do not want to leave here. Especially, I should like to be present at the assault, if there is to be one.

Here, then, extracted from Tolstoy's account of garrison life in Flagstaff Bastion, are expressed the feelings of a Russian officer who was actually serving there at the moment he wrote the words down:

When anyone says, 'I am going to the Fourth Bastion,' a slight agitation or too-marked indifference is always noticeable in him. If men are joking, they say, 'You should be sent to the Fourth Bastion.' No houses, only ruined walls in strange heaps of bricks, boards, clay, and beams. Before you, up a hill, you see a black, untidy space, cut up by ditches. Here, you will meet fewer people and no women at all; soldiers walk briskly by, traces of blood may be seen on the road, and you are sure to meet four soldiers carrying a stretcher, and on the stretcher probably a bloodstained face and a pale overcoat.

Bullets begin to whizz past you, right and left, and you will perhaps consider whether you had better not walk in the trench, which runs parallel to the road. But the trench is full of such yellow, stinking mud, more than knee deep, that you are sure to choose the road. You come to a muddy place, much cut up, surrounded by gabions, cellars, platforms, and dugouts, and on which large cast-iron cannon are mounted, and cannon balls lie piled in orderly heaps. Here, half sunk in mud, lies a shattered cannon, and there a foot soldier is crossing the battery, drawing his feet with difficulty out of the liquid, sticky mud. You hear that awful boom of a shot, which sends a shock all through you.

This is only the Yazonovsky Redoubt, comparatively a very safe and not at all dreadful place. To get to the Fourth Bastion, you must turn to the right along that narrow trench. You may again meet a man with a stretcher, and perhaps a sailor or a soldier with spades. You will see the mouths of mines; dugouts into which only two people can crawl; the same stinking mud, the traces of camp life, and cast-iron refuse of every shape and form.

You will, perhaps, see four or five soldiers, playing cards under the shelter of the breastworks, and a naval officer, noticing you are a stranger, will tell you (but only if you ask) about the bombardment of 5 October – how only one gun in his battery remained usable, and only eight gunners were left out of the whole crew, and how, all the same, the next morning, the sixth, he fired his guns.

He will tell you how a bomb dropped into one of the dugouts, and knocked over eleven sailors; he will show you from an embrasure the enemy's batteries and trenches, which are here not more than 75 yards to 85 yards distant. When you look out of the embrasure, you will be much surprised to find that this whitish stone wall which is so near you, and from which puffs of white smoke keep bursting – that this white wall is the enemy: is *him*, as the soldiers and sailors say.

Very likely, the naval officer will wish to show you some firing. Fourteen sailors, clattering their hobnailed heels on the platform, one putting his pipe in his pocket, quickly and cheerfully man the gun, and begin loading.

Suddenly, the most fearful roar strikes, not only your ears, but your whole being, and makes you shudder all over. It is followed by the whistle of the departing ball, and a thick cloud of powder-smoke envelopes you, the platform, and the moving black figures of the sailors. You will notice their animation, the evidences of a feeling that you had not perhaps expected: the feeling of animosity and thirst for vengeance which lies hidden in each man's soul. You will hear joyful exclamations: *'It's gone right into the embrasure! It's killed two, I think. There – they're carrying them off.'*

'Now, he's riled, and will send one this way,' someone remarks. Soon after, you will see a flash and some smoke. The sentinel, standing on the breastworks, will call out, *'Cannon'* and then a ball will whizz past you and squash into the earth, throwing out a circle of stones and mud. At these sounds, you will experience a strange feeling of mingled pleasure and fear. At the moment the shot is flying towards you, you are sure to imagine that this shot will kill you, but a feeling of pride will support you, and no one will know of the knife that is cutting your heart. But, when the shot has flown past and has not hit you, you revive. A glad, inexpressible joyous feeling seizes you, so that you will feel some peculiar delight in the danger – in this game of life and death – and wish that bombs and balls would fall nearer and nearer to you.

A fall, an explosion, and, mingled with the last, you are startled by the groans of a man. Covered with blood and dirt, he presents a strange, not human, appearance. Part of the sailor's breast has been torn away. 'That's the way with seven or eight every day,' the naval officer remarks to you, answering the look of horror on your face, and he yawns as he rolls another cigarette.

In defiance of the Tsar's secret order that his life should be preserved, and despite his own growing horror at the brutality of war, Second-Lieutenant Tolstoy was happiest when sharing the dangers. The commander-in-chief, Prince Gorchakov, offered to make a staff officer of his young kinsman; Tolstoy refused.

Sent once more to a safe posting in the hills, Tolstoy had time to meditate on what the Crimean War might signify for the Russia of serfdom and secret police. He drew personal conclusions, noting in his diary, 'I must accumulate money, (a) to pay my debts; (b) to free my estate, and make it possible to liberate my serfs.'

A few days before, he had written, 'Is there anything stupider than the 101 shots we fired at the enemy's trenches on the Tsar's birthday?' The war was provoking the best among the Russians to change their loyalties.

Once in a way, even the siege of Sebastopol could have its funny side. There was the case of Prince Oronsov, a chess player of international standing, who was then serving as an officer, and who disliked the unending bloodshed. He seriously proposed to Prince Gorchakov the following plan: Issue a challenge to the English. Let the prize be that coveted trench in front of the 5th Bastion (or, as the enemy choose to call it, the Little Redan). But instead of losing men's lives over the contest for the trench, let the mad English pick their individual champion, and Prince Oronsov would play him for possession of the trench. But at chess.

Leo Tolstoy had begun to relieve his feelings with a bitter humour, too. There was a piano in the officers' mess, around which the young subalterns would gather when off duty, while one of their number hammered out a folk tune. Soon they would all find themselves listening to Count Tolstoy, who had the knack of rattling off impromptu verses – sardonic, satirical, and memorable couplets in which the soldiers' complaints were catchily set down. The young officers' song was overheard by their artillerymen. From thence it spread throughout the army, and soon everyone in Sebastopol was humming Tolstoy's verses.

The improvised folk song recounted the history of the war from Alma onward. It ran something like this:

> In September, the eighth day,
> From the French we ran away
> For our Faith and Tsar,
> For our Faith and Tsar.

The Battle of Alma had been fought on 20 September – but, until 1917, the Russian calendar lagged behind the calendar used by the rest of the world, as if symbolic of Russian backwardness.

> Saint-Arnaud got out of sight,
> And, in a manner most polite,

Came around to our back,
Came around to our back.

Our Liprandi, it is true,
Captured trenches not a few,
But to no avail,
But to no avail.

General Liprandi had commanded at Balaclava, when the
Russians came so close to victory.

'Dannenberg was in command' went on the verse referring
to the defeat at Inkerman – when Dannenberg, then the
supreme commander, had been accused by the Russians
themselves of expending men's lives recklessly.

Dannenberg was in command
Strictly told to understand
Not to spare his men,
Not to spare his men.

Two Grand Dukes a visit paid,
But the French, quite undismayed,
Blazed away with shells,
Blazed away with shells.

Some ten thousand men were shot:
From the Tsar they never got
Any great reward!
Any great reward!

And, in this great battle's flare,
Heroes only two there were:
The two Royal Dukes!
The two Royal Dukes!

This song was traced back from the common soldiers to
Count Leo Tolstoy, who, from that moment on, came under
the suspicion of the 'blues', as the secret political police were
nicknamed. Any hope Tolstoy had of making a successful
official career, in the army or as a civilian, could from now
on be forgotten.

His later descriptions of the siege also express this difference in mood. This is what a visitor found in an exposed bastion later on, when the Allied grip around Sebastopol had tightened, and the Russian dead began to approach one hundred thousand:

Four sailors stood by the breastwork, holding by its arms and legs the bloody corpse of a man without boots and coat, swinging it before heaving it over. (It was impossible, in some parts, to clear away the corpses from the bastions. They were thrown out into the ditch, so as not to be in the way.) Instead of the firing he was used to, amid conditions of perfect exactitude and order, he found two injured mortars, one with its mouth battered in by a ball. He could not get workmen to mend the platform till the morning. Not a single charge was of the weight specified in the Handbook. Two of the men under him were wounded. A gigantic gunner, a seaman who had served with the mortars since the commencement of the siege, by the light of the lantern showed him over the battery as he might over his kitchen garden. The bomb-proof dugout to which his guide led him was an oblong hole, dug in the rocky ground, 25 cubic yards in size, and covered with oak beams, $2\frac{1}{2}$ inches thick.

Only in such dugouts, towards the end, could the lives of men on active service within Sebastopol be sustained. Was an officer class even necessary? 'The N.C.O.s could have done the work just as well without me,' was Tolstoy's opinion of the matter. After the experience in Sebastopol nothing in Russia could ever be quite the same – neither the unquestioning faith of the illiterate private soldier in the Tsar, nor the loyal obedience of the Russian officer himself.

9

Malakoff – a Vast Volcano

SPRING came to the Crimea. Crocuses followed the snow-drops; then came tiny hyacinths. Amid the debris of war, bright vine leaves sprouted. But this springtide there was a significant change in the natural life of the southern Crimea. Flocks bigger than had ever been seen before of ravens, kites, and vultures flapped heavily over last year's battlefields. Some of the vultures had come from as far off as North Africa.

'Things began,' wrote Sergeant Timothy Gowing, 'to look much brighter. We now had plenty of good food, and sickness was on the decrease. We had a few petty annoyances, such as being compelled to pipeclay our belts, so as to make us conspicuous targets for the enemy.'

The British army, by great efforts, had been reinforced to 20,000 men fit for duty. New recruits to the Brigade of Guards had been drilled for sixty days, then sent out to take the place of veterans. The same was true of the Royal Fusiliers. In Gowing's words: 'We now had a great many very young men with us, that had been sent to fill the gaps. We wanted the men that had been sacrificed during the winter, for want of management.' The French army, which at Calamita Bay had been roughly equal to the British, was now at least three times as large. Yet another large French army was being assembled in Constantinople.

Lord Raglan, weary after the strain of the hard winter, was well aware that in the French camp, there was an under-current of intrigue. His advice on running the war was having less and less effect. His opposite number, General Canrobert, appeared nervous and unsure of himself – as though important decisions were being taken somewhere behind his back.

And in fact they were. The Emperor Louis Napoleon, whose military experience had been gained during a brief period of service as a captain in the Swiss army, had decided to come out to the Crimea and take personal command. He had a plan for victory. The newfangled electric telegraph already enabled him to interfere with Canrobert's decisions almost daily. But what the Emperor dreamed of now was leading French armies to victory in person, as his famous uncle had done.

Secret interference from above explains why the first allied onslaught in the spring of 1855 came to grief. The bombardment began on Easter Monday, 9 April, drowning the bells of the Orthodox church inside the fortress city, and the traditional cries of 'Christ is risen!' The French opened fire with 378 guns and mortars, the British with 123. From their beetling, heavily-fortified redoubts, the Russians replied to this fire with a barrage of 466 guns. The ground trembled beneath the feet of the assembled armies, as the firing went on day after day, and the allied infantrymen waiting in the foremost trenches wondered when the order would come to attack.

In Sebastopol's Orthodox church, the chant for the dead now went on night and day. The parqueted floor of the great ballroom, used as a hospital and crowded with Russian wounded, was covered by blood an inch deep. The bombardment cost the besieged Russians 6,000 men.

At a council of war on 13 April Lord Raglan favoured an immediate assault on the battered fortress. But although the military omens were favourable, General Canrobert refused. At another council of war, on 24 April, it was decided to assault Sebastopol on 28 April. Meanwhile, however, Canrobert got word that 20,000 fresh men would probably soon arrive, to be led by the Emperor in person. Sebastopol was ready to be taken by assault, but Canrobert was anxious not to cheat Louis Napoleon of his glory. The cannonade petered out in the vicious but indecisive warfare of bayonet raids on rifle pits, which had gone on at intervals all winter.

That April, Louis Napoleon was invited by Queen Victoria on a state visit to Windsor Castle. He hoped that this visit would, for one thing, establish him, in the eyes of all Europe, as the rightful Emperor of the French. (The Emperor Nicholas, for example, had refused to address Louis Napoleon as 'brother' — the conventional greeting from one monarch to another.) At Windsor, moreover, Louis Napoleon had high hopes, not only of imposing on the allies his plan for victory in the Crimea, but also of getting them to accept him as their commander in the field.

Lord Raglan, when first told of Louis Napoleon's plan, was heard to mutter, 'It appears very complicated.' One army was to invest Sebastopol — entirely surround it — although doing so might cost more in lives than a final assault on the battered fortifications.

A second army, under Lord Raglan was to advance up the valley of the River Tchernaya, and cut Sebastopol off completely from the Russian field army. But what if the Russians, for once, gained the upper hand in the pitched battle that was bound to result? The consequences of the plan, in Lord Raglan's view, had not been thought out.

A third army, meanwhile, called the Army of Diversion, numbering 60,000 men, exclusively French and commanded by Louis Napoleon in person, would attack Sebastopol from the north. How this army was to cross the broad estuary of Sebastopol harbour under the devastating fire of Russian naval guns was never explained. The allies so far had not made a great success of synchronizing their military actions, even though they had spent most of the war within shouting distance of each other. Three widely separated armies, marching to the whims of a former Swiss artillery captain, seemed to Lord Raglan a recipe for disaster.

The Emperor's plan to lead this army in person was finally voted upon during his state visit by a council of war that met in Windsor Castle. Louis Napoleon's ears still rang with the loud hurrahs of loyal British subjects who had lined the streets to catch a glimpse of him. He had been driven magnificently through London – the city where, not so long ago, he had lived as a shiftless, shabby exile, unable to pay his debts. Now, the faces around him of statesmen and soldiers and royal princes were respectful and deferential. They were all treating the adventurer as if he were truly Emperor.

After a discussion, the bold frankness of which came as a shock for an emperor used to the flattery that fear inspires, the council of war took a vote. Lord Panmure, the British War Minister, voted against the Emperor's taking personal command. So did the Prince Consort, representing Queen Victoria. So did shrewd, hardheaded Lord Palmerston, whom Louis Napoleon had always counted on, politically, as his consistent friend. Lord Hardinge, the one-armed veteran who was British Commander-in-Chief (he had succeeded Wellington in 1852), voted against, and even Marshal Vaillant, the French Minister of War, was encouraged by the support he was getting from the British to make a firm stand. The Emperor might be able to dismiss his minister with a stroke of the pen, but he could not so easily shrug off the British alliance.

General Canrobert, totally demoralized by the difficulty of pleasing the Emperor and at the same time running the war, sent in his resignation in the following words: 'My health and my mind, fatigued by constant tension, no longer allow me to carry the burden of an immense responsibility. I ask the Emperor to leave me a combatant's place at the head of a simple division.'

General Pélissier, a stocky, corpulent, heavy-moustached, rough-mannered Norman, aged sixty-one, was now, to universal relief, given the French supreme command. 'Pélissier was known to be a most resolute man,' wrote Sergeant Gowing. 'Our men cheered heartily, throwing their caps in the air.' Pélissier was not a man to be afraid of responsibility, or anything else whatever.

On 8 May, some odd-looking troops arrived. There were 5,000 of them, and they went up-country to strengthen the allied front along the River Tchernaya. The best of them, the Bersaglieri, wore distinctive plumes of cock's feathers at the side of their hats. They spoke Italian, and their general was called Della Marmora. Troops of the Kingdom of Sardinia had come to play their part in the Crimean fighting.

And what quarrel had the King of Sardinia with the Emperor of All the Russias? None whatever.

The policy of the Kingdom of Sardinia was, however, in the hands of a singularly clever minister, Count Cavour. His great ambition was to have his king, Victor Emmanuel II, one day reign over a united Italy. Being useful to France and Britain might bring this day closer. The Allies needed soldiers? Sardinia could supply them.

After this war, there would be need for a treaty that might somehow restore to Europe the balance of power that had secured peace for forty years. Having fought in the war, the Sardinians would have a right to be represented at the conference table. The Austrians, the oppressors of Italy, would not. Of all the troops serving in the Crimea, none were more simply the pawns of statesmen playing their game of power than those bronzed, sun-loving Bersaglieri, swaggering under their cock's-feather plumes.

The telegraph station in the Crimea was near the site of the ancient Greek temple of Artemis. Cheated of personal command, General Pélissier patiently made his plans for another assault on the city, in early summer, though he knew Louis Napoleon disapproved.

His telegram to the Emperor, announcing this intended attack, was so businesslike as almost to be insolently curt: I AM GOING TO SEE LORD RAGLAN, WHO SHARES MY IDEAS, IN ORDER TO SETTLE THE LAST DISPOSITIONS FOR THE ATTACK BY

STORM, WHICH OUGHT TO PLACE IN OUR POWER THE WHITE WORK, THE MAMELON [a strong outwork of the Malakoff] AND THE QUARRY BEFORE THE REDAN. The Emperor's reply was sharp: I GIVE YOU A POSITIVE ORDER NOT TO DEVOTE YOURSELF TO THE SIEGE BEFORE HAVING INVESTED THE PLACE.

General Pélissier, compelled to choose, did not for a moment hesitate. The French army would attack the outer works of Sebastopol in June, in defiance of the Emperor's direct order. If victorious, well and good – but what if Pélissier failed?

The allied cannonade, this time by 450 big guns, opened on 6 June and lasted for six days. Colonel Todleben (soon to be seriously wounded) noted now the slowness of fire of the British guns was made up for by their remarkable precision of aim. By 10 June the Russians had lost 3,500 men under this bombardment, the allies 750, and the north face of the dominating Malakoff Redoubt was silenced.

During the night of 7 June the French grouped their men for the hazardous preliminary attack on the Mamelon – the chief outwork of the mighty Malakoff. The attack would be led by Zouaves and Green Chasseurs, crack troops renowned for their dash and vigour. When the time came, they drove back Russian sharpshooters, under the personal command of Vice Admiral Nakhimov.

Following the Zouaves, the centre column of the French attack, the 50th Regiment of the Line, led by Colonel Brancion, went directly up the slope of the Mamelon and managed to cross the ditch. The French infantry worked their way into the Mamelon, said W. H. Russell, who watched it all, 'like a clever pack of hounds'. Colonel Brancion was shot dead, but his men poured in after him, and soon the *Tricolore* rose in triumph above the Mamelon's walls.

Advanced detachments of the French, dashing forward, had even pressed their attack to the battered, heavy white tower of the Malakoff itself, but the Russian infantry, sallying out boldly, drove them back.

The Mamelon was an outwork correctly fortified, so that

only the side facing the allied lines gave protection. Colonel Todleben had left it wide open to the rear, so that if one day the Mamelon should fall to the enemy, they would be exposed to Russian fire from the Malakoff itself. Galled by this gunfire, the French worked like demons all night, and by dawn had a trench dug across this open stretch, to complete the ring of fortification. The Mamelon Redoubt was newly named the Brancion Redoubt. The French infantry had now established a foothold only fifty yards from the great strong point, Malakoff, which was the key to all Sebastopol.

The Mamelon, already torn up by the artificial earthquake of gunfire, had been planted by the Russians with fougasses. These were ingenious mines. The pressure of a soldier's foot would break a buried glass tube, so that sulphuric acid ran down to explode a potassium-chlorate detonator. The hidden explosive charge would send flaming bitumen flying into the air, to burn where it did not kill outright: not quite napalm, but scientific warfare was taking its first strides.

The *Tricolore* hoisted over the Mamelon had been the signal agreed for the British assault on the Quarries — a similar outwork confronting the Redan. This outwork, also, since not enclosed on the fortress side, gave no cover from Russian fire once captured. The British attacked this work on each flank, with 700 men of the Light and 2nd Divisions, under Colonel Shirley, and 600 in close support — a handful, compared with the mass attack that had carried the French into the Mamelon.

Sergeant Gowing, of the Royal Fusiliers, was once more in the thick of it:

We were told off to take the Quarries. Our bayonets were soon in the midst of them. It was rough hitting for about half an hour; it was a little piece of work well done.

Our people set to work with pick and shovel as hard as men could work, but the enemy came on repeatedly, with strong columns, and tried to retake them. The fighting then became desperate. The enemy were three or four to one. We ran short of ammunition, and then we were in a nice mess. We used stones, as we did at Inkerman, and as soon as they came close enough we went at them with that ugly bit of cold steel. At times we were under such a fire of grape and musketry, that it appeared impossible for anything to live.

Some fourteen times they were hurled back, with terrible slaughter; we were now under good cover, the pick and shovel having been at it all night. Our loss had been heavy – the Quarries were afterwards well named the Shambles.

The British and French were now well placed for a final assault on the city's key redoubts. The French capture of the Mamelon had been proof of skill and high courage. Yet, for seven days after, no word of congratulation came over the dreaded electric wire from Paris.

At last the Emperor, still obsessed with his vague dreams of military glory, sent Pélissier this cold comment on the French losses, which so far numbered 5,440: A GENERAL ACTION WHICH WOULD HAVE DECIDED THE FATE OF THE CRIMEA WOULD HAVE COST MORE.

Knowing he deserved better than that, General Pélissier telegraphed the following reply:

THE COMPLETION OF YOUR ORDERS IS IMPOSSIBLE. IT IS TO PLACE ME, SIRE, BETWEEN INSUBORDINATION AND DISCREDIT. I PRAY YOUR MAJESTY EITHER TO FREE ME FROM THE STRAITENED LIMITS IMPOSED ON ME, OR TO PERMIT ME TO RESIGN A COMMAND IMPOSSIBLE TO EXERCISE, IN CONCERT WITH MY LOYAL ALLIES, AT THE END, SOMETIMES PARALYSING, OF AN ELECTRIC WIRE.

Pélissier was risking his career, perhaps even his freedom, in taking this tone. To speak like this, one must be morally sure of victory, and Pélissier, as it happened, was close at that moment to defeat. The harassment of the Emperor's telegraphic interference had trapped him into two errors of judgement that were seriously to mar his plans.

That cold telegram from the Emperor, when all the Army awaited praise, became known to Pélissier's rivals among the senior French generals. Bosquet, a popular commander, had reasonable expectations of perhaps succeeding Pélissier. He committed a foolish action, which his commander-in-chief might have been right to consider treacherous. General Bosquet, who had already criticized Pélissier's plan of attack, now held back a captured Russian plan of the Malakoff Redoubt, instead of forwarding the valuable piece of intelligence rapidly.

General Péllissier did not dare tolerate such an insubordinate act. So it came about that within thirty-six hours of the final assault, General Bosquet, who knew the ground and had the full confidence of his troops, was summarily removed from his command. The man who took his place, Regnaud de St Jean Angély, had only just arrived from Paris.

Pélissier's second error of judgement was more disastrous yet.

Experience had taught the allies how, even after the heaviest bombardment, the Russians could usually manage to get their dismounted cannon firing again overnight. Now, the allied cannonade on 17 June 1855 had completely silenced the redoubts to be attacked next day. The assault was timed for the eighteenth, which happened to be the fortieth anniversary of the Battle of Waterloo, and was to be preceded by another two-hour cannonade. This had been formally agreed with Lord Raglan – but, at the last moment, General Pélissier impatiently cancelled his morning bombardment, so that the French troops could more conveniently mass at their assembly points under cover of darkness.

But, from as early as 2 a.m., all his troops' movements had been observed by the Russians. By dawn, their guns opened a terribly destructive fire, from almost point-blank range, on the massed French columns.

To put a final touch to this day of disaster, the general commanding the French left mistook the agreed signal, and led his men out too soon, into an overwhelming hail of Russian fire from the ramparts. Although the French had brought together the huge total of 25,000 men for their assault, it all petered out in a futile and costly exchange of rifle fire between Frenchmen on the ground, and Russians on the parapets. No one could live long in no-man's-land under that devastating cannonade.

As dawn broke, Lord Raglan himself was watching this French fiasco from a dangerously exposed advanced trench in the British front line. Forty years ago to the day, he had lost his right arm at Waterloo. Lord Raglan was now under hot fire from grape shot – bullets the size of small apples, piled symmetrically around a spindle until they fit the bore of the gun. The spindle comes on separately, whirring like a partridge.

He could see how this bombardment of grape shot, lobbed into the trenches, was already beginning to chop up his infantry crouching there under cover. Out in no-man's-land, it was worse. Yet to hold back at this moment would betray his hard-pressed allies – and Lord Raglan, all through the long campaign, had shown a perfect fidelity to the Anglo-French alliance. He had invariably kept his word, even though it might mean suffering the whims of a dying man, like Saint-Arnaud, or the duplicities of a political general like Canrobert. To let Pélissier down at a moment like this was unthinkable.

Lord Raglan, sick at heart, gave the order for the British to attack, though he knew his men would move out of those trenches into certain annihilation.

Sergeant Gowing, who went over the top with his company of the Royal Fusiliers, described the fire from Malakoff as being 'like a vast volcano'. He watched his colonel climb the parapet and go out in front, sword in one hand, newfangled Colt revolver in the other. Both colonel and adjutant were almost at once shot down by the diabolical cross fire.

The survivors of the Royal Fusiliers pushed on across the shell-torn ground, alongside a party of seamen carrying ladders to raise against the city walls. At the *chevaux-de-frise* – the outer barricade of the redoubt – when they still had fifty yards to go, the Fusiliers and bluejackets were met, from enemy guns fired point-blank, according to Sergeant Gowing, by:

a perfect hell of fire, grape, shot, shell, canister and musketry, and could not return a shot. The 'retire' was sounded all over the field, but the men were sullen, and would not heed it. At last, the remnant of the attacking column retired to their trenches, amidst a storm of grape which nearly swept away whole companies at a time.

Afterwards, the Russians flew the black flag, and fired on the wounded. We had what might be called a good sound drubbing. Our people are not good hands at putting up with much of that; officers and men wanted to 'go it again', but we had to obey orders.

Sergeant Gowing himself had no fewer than nine holes shot through trousers, coat, and cap. Of his company of Fusiliers, which that morning had comprised one captain, two lieutenants, four sergeants, four corporals, two drummer boys, and ninety men, only Sergeant Gowing and thirteen men survived. The third company of his battalion came back with nine men out of ninety-six. In half an hour, mainly through Pélissier's having underrated the Russian capacity to get their guns firing overnight yet again, the allies had lost 7,988 men.

Twelve days later, old Lord Raglan died − officially of mild cholera; but those close to him held it was from a broken heart. Tough General Pélissier, who knew he had lost a good friend, wept like a child for over an hour at Raglan's deathbed.

The British general who replaced Lord Raglan, a General James Simpson, was not the man the British army would have chosen, and did little to distinguish himself. With Lord Raglan gone, the British in the Crimea were henceforward to play second fiddle to General Pélissier's French, whose numbers and aggressiveness and prowess grew daily. Inside Sebastopol, Vice Admiral Nakhimov died of wounds on 10

July. Colonel Todleben, severely wounded on 20 June, soon after left the city he had fortified.

When the Russians had run down their black flag, and at last flown a white flag, indicating that they agreed to a burial truce, the officers they sent over to supervise their men were exquisitely turned out. To impress allied officers that Sebastopol lacked for nothing, they wore white kid gloves and patent leather boots and clean linen. Their brave bluff, however, deceived no one. From 18 July onward, the allies took note how the Russians had begun to lose heart for sorties against the advanced posts that now were encroaching upon the city walls. Asked when he proposed to renew the assault, General Pélissier answered cynically, 'Well, I don't know: the Russians are losing every day 300 to 400 men by sickness. If we wait a week, they will have lost a brigade; if we wait a month, they will have lost a division.'

The Emperor still wanted the issue to be settled in a pitched battle. Over the telegraph, Pélissier argued, BEFORE THE FORTRESS, OUR FAILURES DO NOT CHANGE THE SITUATION; THEY LEAVE US WHERE WE WERE YESTERDAY. The French could afford to try and try again until they forced a way into Sebastopol.

Pélissier was correct about the size of the Russian losses. At the burial truce, one Russian officer, losing his self-control, had suddenly burst out, 'Losses! You don't know what the word means; you should see our batteries; the dead lie there in heaps and heaps. Troops cannot live under such a fire of hell as you poured upon us.' From March to August 1855 the Russians were to lose 81,000 men, killed and wounded, in and around Sebastopol.

All now depended on how well General Pélissier could resist imperial pressure. His June assault had been a costly failure. The demand that he meet the Russians in the open somewhere up-country became more vocal. The Russians, too, were beginning to think that it might pay them to fight a pitched battle. A defeat in the field, by cutting off the Allies from their sea bases, might leave them helpless.

Pélissier's information was that up in the hills the enemy were bringing together food, horses, and guns, in the hope of a last breakthrough – one final attempt to drive the foreign invaders back into the sea.

10

'For Ever' — or Fourteen Years

FRENCH Chasseurs on patrol had brought word that Russians were massing in the hill country beyond the valley of the River Tchernaya. The right wing under General Read totalled 13,000 infantry, 2,000 cavalry, and 62 guns. Their left was commanded by General Liprandi, who had brought the Russians almost to the sea on the day when only the thin red line of Highlanders held them back from Balaclava Bay. The Russian left numbered 16,000 infantry and 70 guns. A Russian infantry reserve, stationed to the rear, totalled 18,000 men and was supported by 36 guns. A cavalry reserve of 8,000 with 28 guns of horse artillery, was waiting to push a way through any gap that might open in the allied defensive line. The long-awaited pitched battle was soon due.

To sharp-eyed Second-Lieutenant Count Leo Tolstoy, serving with the guns, this huge Russian army looked less awe-inspiring than it might to a mounted Chasseur, spying on the enemy from a safe distance. The latest Russian recruits, as he could see, were no better than local militia. Even vast Russia was coming to the end of her cannon fodder. Many private soldiers were in rags, or had marched their way through the soles of their boots.

Nor did the preparations for battle impress. A letter was read aloud from the new Tsar, Alexander II, reminding the men of their valour last year at the Battle of Balaclava. Now any old soldier who had fought there, and lived through the terrible winter to tell the tale, knew perfectly well that Balaclava was not a real victory. The Russians may have captured some British guns, but they were driven back from

136

their objectives. After the Tsar's letter had been read, each soldier, before going into action, was presented with a large bottle of brandy.

General Pélissier's plan had a confident obstinacy, typical of the man himself – a strong-willed Norman of peasant stock. To confront the allies, he knew the Russians would need somehow to cross the Tchernaya River. If they planned to come down the road to Balaclava, they would be obliged to cross the river at or near a stone bridge called the Traktir Bridge. Here Pélissier concentrated his artillery. The 40,000 men, French, Turks and Sardinians, posted in readiness along the line of the Tchernaya, had dug themselves in. The bank nearest the Russians was lightly held by outposts of crack troops – Bersaglieri and Zouaves. The stone bridge itself was left intact, like the bait in a trap.

The Russian attack began at reveillé on 16 August 1855 when the allied outposts, in bivouac, had lighted fires to prepare their coffee. A brisk cannonade announced the onset, and soon after there appeared the familiar grey-coated massed Russian columns. Zouaves and Bersaglieri were driven back across the bridge – but they had given useful warning. The allied army was poised in readiness on the low hills beyond.

After the summer drought, the River Tchernaya was, in fact, shallow enough to be forded; but, as the foremost Russian soldiers reached the bank, they flung themselves down and began to drink. The Tsar's gift of brandy had given them an unbearable thirst. Watching and waiting on the hills above, the allied soldiers could observe far off the morning sun glitter on the polished helmets and sabres of the enormous Russian cavalry reserve – far out of range, restlessly alert.

Along the foot of the line of low hills where the Allies had dug in, there ran a steep-banked aqueduct, taking water to Sebastopol. Where it skirted the foot of the hill, this ten-foot-high embankment gave the Russians momentary cover. Once they moved clear of the aqueduct and started up the steep, bare, sun-dried slope, they became targets for a terrible concentration of gunfire. Their first blind rush uphill lasted no longer than ten minutes. The Russian vanguard broke and ran, only to be checked in its flight by the second attacking wave. Their comrades, coming on from behind, bore them forward once again, willy-nilly, towards the zone of danger.

Russians of the 5th Brigade of Light Artillery had heroically manhandled two of their guns across the stone bridge under fire. They were beginning to sweep the road and the heights beyond, so as to back up their advancing infantry. The second wave got as far as halfway up the bare, corpse-strewn hill before the scientific French cannonade overwhelmed them and drove them back.

Another Russian column, attacking the French right, was being held in an infilading fire by Sardinian artillery, and systematically cut to pieces. Hillside, aqueduct and riverbed were filled by now with grey-clad Russians. The stone arches of the Traktir Bridge were so choked with corpses that the flowing water, as it rose against this obstruction, had begun to flood the river valley on either side.

For a third time the Russians, by the costly method of blind frontal attack, tried to force their way down the Balaclava road. On the far side of the bridge, they rounded up survivors from the previous attacks – men maddened by brandy and tormented by thirst. The broken formations of these survivors were stiffened with infantry from the reserve, and came across the River Tchernaya past the tumbled bodies of their own dead for yet a third time. On the bare ground of that shot-infested hillside the Russian attack once more wavered and broke.

As their grey-coated infantry ran for their lives, out came three Russian batteries, each of twelve guns, and began systematically, effectively, to cover their comrades' retreat. The entire army was moving off the way it had come. By ten o'clock that morning, only black lines, like columns of moving ants, and a huge, distant cloud of dust showed in the far distance. The Russians, in those few hours of cannonade, had lost 3 generals, 66 officers, and 23,000 men. Pélissier let the retreating army go. Whatever his imperial master might think, it was not his business to be lured, even by victory, into fighting a campaign in the barren interior.

Leo Tolstoy's growing awareness that the government of the Tsar was corrupt, and the Russian cause in the Crimea close to defeat, did not discourage him, after the battle, from volunteering at once for service inside Sebastopol. Now that Nakhimov was dead and Todleben wounded, Tolstoy's kinsman Prince Gorchakov had personally taken over command of the siege. Even before Second-Lieutenant Tolstoy arrived there, Prince Gorchakov, after his first tour of inspection, had written gloomily but candidly to his Tsar, 'There is not a man in the army who would not call it folly to continue the defence any longer.'

There was, in fact, no longer a city to defend, only a heap of rubble and cinders. There were not enough sandbags to protect the guns. Mortar fire from the allied lines, which went on roaring blindly all night, chopped to pieces the dwindling band of men who laboured in darkness to make operational, once more, the Russian guns dismounted the previous day. Survivors lived packed like sardines in caves and dugouts beneath the parapets. Around the guns, dead gunners lay in heaps. There were not even enough men left alive to carry off the wounded.

Prince Gorchakov, having made up his mind to abandon the city, gave orders for a bridge of boats to be built, directly across the harbour, to where Star Fort defended the northern shore. Until the very moment of withdrawal, the outer line of famous bastions would be held. Those who tried to force their way into Sebastopol could still get hurt. Barricades were built across the streets, buildings were boobytrapped with fougasses, and all the powder magazines were mined, to be blown up when the signal was given.

*

The Russians obstinately clinging to their outer redoubts could see clearly the difference in scale between the French and British assaulting parties.

General Pélissier concentrated a grand total of 36,000 Frenchmen to assault the Malakoff Redoubt, and had another 10,000 available in reserve. General Simpson chose to bring up less than a thirtieth of that number – 1,380 men – for his misconceived final attack on the Redan.

Tolstoy describes how he saw the fall of the city from a point of vantage near the signal telegraph at Star Fort. He and a companion were watching the clouds of smoke, and gun flashes, through a telescope. The September day was gloomy, with an autumnal nip in the air; a reminder that with winter close, the Allies dared dally no longer. The two young officers began listening anxiously for an answering fire from Russian guns.

'The Second Bastion does not reply at all, now.'

'The Malakoff sends hardly one shot, in reply to three of theirs.'

'They are shooting straight into the Kornilov Battery, and it does not reply.'

'They always stop the bombardment about noon. Come, let's go to lunch.'

'Wait a bit!'

'What is it? What?'

'A movement in the trenches. Thick columns advancing.'

On the bastions, white cloudlets burst in succession, as if chasing one another. The wind brought a sound of rapid small-arms firing, like the beating of rain against a window. Puffs of smoke rose more and more often, and at last formed one lilac cloud, which kept curling and uncurling, and all the sounds blent into one tremendous clatter.

'An assault!'

Cossacks galloped along the road, some officers rode by, the commander-in-chief passed in his carriage with his suite.

'It's impossible they can have taken it!'

'My God – a standard. Look. Look. A French standard on the Malakoff!'

Soon, the entire Russian garrison began marching in column across the bridge of boats to the north shore, leaving behind them the deserted shell of a fortress city. As each soldier reached the far side, he crossed himself.

Colonel Charles Windham, known for the rest of his life by the nickname of 'Redan' Windham, had two nights before tossed a coin with Colonel Uniet, to decide which of them should have the honour of leading the British assault party on the other great Russian redoubt. Having won the toss, Colonel Windham spent the night before the attack writing to his wife, to suggest how she might apply for a pension, and arranging his other personal affairs in the cool and certain expectation of death.

Lieutenant Ranken, of the Royal Engineers, was not too optimistic, either. He decided to wear his red shell jacket, the article of uniform that made an officer look most like a ranker, so as to reduce his chances of being picked off by a Russian sharpshooter.

At 1 p.m., amid the deafening din of bombardment, Colonel Windham drew his sword, and went manfully over the parapet of the outermost British trench, followed by infantrymen of the 41st Regiment, with Grenadiers following. The British had a stretch of open ground to cross much wider than no-man's-land between Russians and French. Moreover, General Simpson's plan of attack had sent them up against the Redan at a point where the looming walls formed a salient, which created a trap, since Russians could keep up a cross fire from confronting walls. The British reserves had been left an hour's march to the rear. Colonel Windham was right to feel gloomy about his chances.

Most important of all, the men following Charles Windham lacked the aggressive confidence of that highly trained army that had been sacrificed during the previous winter. Although Sergeant Timothy Gowing, on the spot as usual, observed that some old Inkerman veterans went into action coolly puffing their clay pipes, he noted also that 'there were in our ranks a great number of very young men, many only sixteen, some with only two months service.' It was even found, at one point in the heat of action, that one young British soldier did not know how to fire off his rifle.

The outer ditch defending the Redan was twenty feet deep. The men behind Colonel Windham could be seen entering this ditch briskly enough, and coming up the other side, but they clung to the cover afforded by the ditch, and went into the salient only in driblets. Many, when they got there, lay down behind rubble to return the Russian fire – which, though better than nothing, was not the real job of an assault party.

The raw recruits near Windham had begun to speak of their mortal fear that the Redan might be mined. Colonel Windham himself, so far miraculously unscathed, had sent back message after message to headquarters, insisting that supports be sent up at once. Only a mass attack, in the French style, would stand the remotest chance of pushing all the way into the Redan. But each young officer sent back by Windham with this urgent demand was shot down crossing the bleak and bare terrain of no-man's-land.

A group of British did manage to cling closely to the redoubt for as long as an hour – but when Windham had decided there was nothing for it but to go back for reinforcements in person, a Russian sortie at bayonet point succeeded in driving the last of the attacking party away from the walls of the Redan.

General Pélissier then asked General Simpson formally if he intended to renew the assault on the redoubt, which, though it might never succeed, at least would take some pressure off the French. Though the Guards and Highlanders, as well as his third and Fourth Divisions, had not yet been engaged, General Simpson replied that he did not feel in a condition to do so. (Soon after, General Simpson was relieved of his command, and replaced, though too late, by Sir William Codrington, who had fought with the Light Division all the way from Calamita Bay.)

The British camp was deeply depressed by this failure. The assault was to be renewed the next day before dawn, at 5 a.m. – but, during the night, British volunteers, crawling between the lines and up to the enemy embrasures, found the Redan deserted. Sebastopol was already abandoned. For the British, the war had ended ingloriously.

As they went, the Russians hurried to complete the destruction of their great naval base, which allied bombardments had begun. All ships of war remaining in the harbour were set on fire, as were those buildings that remained intact in the devastated city itself. Fort Alexander blew up with a stupendous crash. Four immense explosions announced the final destruction of Quarantine Fort, and of the magazines and batteries in Central Bastion and Flagstaff Fort. As the allies entered the city, they were greeted by clouds of smoke, and showers of stone and timber. They had captured a ruin.

At least three hundred thousand Russians, perhaps more, had met their death within the city, and in the successive battles on the Crimean upland. Uncounted hundreds of thousands had succumbed before they ever met an enemy, during the winter marches across the endless Russian plains. Inside Sebastopol, one place of burial alone was named by the soldiers the Cemetery of the Hundred Thousand.

For a while, after her mauling in the Crimean Campaign, Russia ceased to be so feared in Europe by countries whose freedom she had threatened to blot out only a few years before. Russian social and economic backwardness had been exposed in the eyes of the civilized world.

The freeing of the serfs was only one among a number of political reforms that now had become inevitable; Leo Tolstoy's generation of educated Russians, marked by the harsh lessons of the Crimea, were to play a great part in seeing these necessary changes carried through.

Meanwhile, that September morning, as they assembled on the north shore of Sebastopol's harbour, the Russians were far from defeated. Prince Gorchakov had under his command an army ragged and weary, but still capable of organized resistance. Nor, with winter coming on, were the Allies in good shape to pursue the war into the interior of Russia, though this was the plan of action advocated by Louis Napoleon. He had apparently forgotten what a Russian winter did to the army of his famous uncle in 1812. The wily Pélissier (soon to be ennobled as Duc de Malakoff) was by no means to be tempted out of sight of the ships that fed his men.

Negotiations for a peace were long drawn out. Meanwhile, the British army lived through a second winter on the shores of Balaclava Bay – this time in a comfortable hutted camp, with warm clothing and abundant rations, and modern hospital facilities.

The Treaty of Paris, signed on 30 March 1856, laid down that the naval dockyard of Sebastopol should be abolished 'for ever'. Warships of all nations were excluded from the Black Sea. Russia agreed to respect the Danubian Principalities, which later became Rumania. This political result may seem insignificant, compared with the price paid for it in lives.

'For ever', as the Russians understood the term, lasted this time about fourteen years. In 1870, during the Franco–Prussian War, which ended in a German occupation of Paris, they denounced the treaty, since they knew the French were far too busy to object. In 1890, Tsar Alexander III launched a large new Russian warship from the rebuilt dockyard at Sebastopol. The name chosen for it had a certain cynically bullying overtone: *Sinop*, after the Russians' bombardment of the Turkish Fleet thirty-seven years before.

What other alterations, large and small, can be traced back to the Crimean War?

When the bearded military heroes came back to Victorian London puffing their pipes, they set a decisive change in fashion: pipes and beards were now symbols of manliness. A station on the Paris Métro is still called Malakoff. A public house in Queensway, London, is called The Redan. From the assortment of odd clothes experimented with by the British, to withstand exposure in that terrible first winter, two or three male garments have survived: the cardigan, a knitted and buttoned jacket, named after the Noble Yachtsman; and the raglan sleeve, as used on overcoats favoured by the one-armed British commander-in-chief, well known for his fantastic taste in clothes. There is also a head covering – a knitted hood – which is called a balaclava helmet.

There were more serious changes, too. After those four decades of unbroken peace, when the British navy had successfully policed the world, the Crimean Campaign once again introduced into Europe the idea of scientific and aggressive war. Victory made Louis Napoleon's dictatorship slightly more acceptable to the French – or slightly harder to shake off. By isolating Austria diplomatically, the war accelerated the rise of Prussian military power. Such notorious fiascos as the Charge of the Light Brigade weakened, though they did not break, the grip of the aristocracy on the British army. British military hospitals have never again been quite so much like hell on earth. The effects of this war, as of all wars, rippled further and further outward, like sea waves after a distant submarine disaster.

Perhaps the real moral to be drawn from the Crimean Campaign is that any war between an elephant and a whale is likely to be inconclusive, and certain to be unwise.

Further Reading

A. W. Kinglake's *Invasion of the Crimea* (Blackwood, 1877–78) is a long, slow, and enormously detailed account of the campaign from a British point of view, up to the death of Lord Raglan. Kinglake, who could write cogently when the need arose, set out to save the face of the British army, not by hiding mistakes – that was impossible – but by burying every happening under such a mass of insignificant but authenticated fact that no one could see daylight. It's like watching a film of a war in very slow motion. Baring Pemberton's *The Battles of the Crimea* (Batsford, 1961) speeds up and adds colour to Kinglake's account.

General Sir Edward Hamley's *War in the Crimea* (Seeley, 1891) is a balanced professional account by an experienced military historian, who checked Russian and French sources, and tried to be fair to all sides. As a general, he is, of course, tempted to be kind, whenever possible, to the generals.

A more recent general history, which skilfully illuminates the political and diplomatic background to the war, is C. E. Vulliamy's *Crimea* (Cape, 1939).

W. H. Russell's famous dispatches from the Crimea to London *Times* were reprinted, with some editing, in *The War* (Routledge, 1855–6). A useful and interesting selection from the original dispatches was made by Nicholas Bentley in *Russell's Despatches from the Crimea* (Deutsch, 1966). Journalism is not often as alive as this even now – a hundred years later.

Sergeant Timothy Gowing's *A Voice from the Ranks*, which

gives an autobiographical account of his varied military career, has been edited and abridged by K. Fenwick for the Folio Society (1959), with special emphasis on the Crimea.

Leo Tolstoy's *Sebastopol* (Cresset, 1961) is available in a number of translations into English.

Kellow Chesney, in *The Crimean War Reader* (Muller, 1960) has gathered quotations from many contemporary documents and memoirs. Several British soldiers who fought there wrote interestingly afterwards. Sir Evelyn Wood, who served as a midshipman with the ladder party assaulting the Redan, later wrote *From Midshipman to Fieldmarshal* (Methuen, 1906). Sir Charles Windham's *Crimean Diary* appeared in 1897 (Paul), and G. Ranken's *Six Months at Sabastopol* in 1857. Mrs Henry Duberly, the wife of an officer, followed the army to the very brink of action, and wrote a high-spirited *Journal of the Russian War* (London, 1856). The Reverend S. G. Osborne, chaplain at Scutari, launched the Florence Nightingale legend with his *Scutari and Its Hospitals* (London, 1855).

The liveliest and most illuminating modern books on the Crimea are by C. Woodham Smith. Granted access to family papers, she has written, in *The Reason Why* (Constable, 1956; Penguin, 1958), an interesting and vivid account of the conflict of personality between Cardigan and Lucan, which led to the Charge of the Light Brigade. Her brilliant *Florence Nightingale* (Constable, 1950) will remain the standard biography.

Index

Also in Puffins

THE BOER WAR

by James Barbary

Often a fair-minded account of a war can be written only long after the fighting is over. Here is just such a history of the Boer War. It tells a story of courage, ignorance and mistaken beliefs – of the human strength and weakness shown by individual leaders on both sides. Many famous men were involved – Kitchener, Jan Smuts, Baden-Powell, Paul Kruger, Winston Churchill, Lord Roberts, Cecil Rhodes. Some won fame, others did harm to their own good repute. The Boers were amateur soldiers, and developed many ways of fighting that were then unusual in war. They became experts at guerilla warfare – their small mobile forces attacked swiftly and then disappeared into a countryside they knew better than the enemy. The British fought back with a 'scorched earth' policy, and held many thousands of prisoners in their concentration camps – the 'invention' of Lord Kitchener.

THE BOER WAR tells of a conflict where more people were killed by sickness than by bullets, and women and children suffered as much as the soldiers; it goes on to show how the compromises of the peace treaty helped to bring about the problems South Africa faces to this day.

TO BE A SLAVE
by Julius Lester

Can you imagine what it must have been like to be a slave?
Can you think of yourself as being owned by somebody else,
just as you might own a dog, or a bicycle or a table or chair?
As a slave you had no rights of any kind. Your owner could
sell you if he wished, separating you from your wife, or
husband, or home, or child, completely as the whim took him.

This book tells you what it must have been like. It is con-
structed from the memories of ex-slaves taken from the
records of the American Anti-Slavery Society and many
other Northern abolition groups, recorded both before and
after the American Civil War, and the excerpts are linked
together by Julius Lester into a history of the Black Americans.

THE DODO, THE AUK AND THE ORYX
by Robert Silverberg

'As dead as a dodo' is a sadly common expression. Sad because no one in living memory has ever seen a dodo, and the
world is a sadder place for it. But how many other creatures
have we driven, or are we driving, to extinction?

In the fifty years between 1851 and 1901 thirty-one kinds
of mammal disappeared, and today about 600 forms of
animal life are near vanishing point. Robert Silverberg
tells the story of some of these birds and beasts which have
vanished from the earth and others which have been rescued
from extinction, or rediscovered when they were thought to
have disappeared forever. Today we are making some effort
to preserve our wild life: it is worth preserving. Just imagine
how dull the world would be without tigers, elephants,
humming-birds, aardvarks and kangaroos!

THE BOOMERANG BOOK

by M. J. Hanson

Do you know how to make a boomerang bounce? Can you throw it so that it circles a tree or post and then returns to you? Can you make it fly back past you and return to you?

In this book M. J. Hanson tells you how to make and throw your own boomerangs. He gives clear step-by-step instructions for both right-handed and left-handed boomerang throwers and with a little patience and a little woodwork skill you will produce a boomerang that will make you the envy of your friends.

Join the ancient art of boomerang throwing. It's fun, it's cheap and it's catching!

THE PAPER AEROPLANE BOOK

by Seymour Simon

What makes paper aeroplanes soar and plummet, loop and glide? Why do they fly at all?

This book will show you how to make them and explains why they do the things they do. Making paper aeroplanes is fun and, by following the author's step-by-step instructions and doing the simple experiments he suggests, you will also discover what makes a real aeroplane fly. As you make and fly paper planes of different designs, you will learn about lift, thrust, drag and gravity; you will see how wing size and shape, and fuselage weight and balance, affect the lift of a plane; how ailerons, elevators and the rudder work to make a plane dive or climb, loop or glide, roll or spin. Once you have grasped these principles of flight, you will be ready to take off with designs of your own.

EXPLORERS

A series of non-fiction titles for children between 10 and 12
years of age, Explorers are readable, informative and visually
exciting. Explorers are 48 pages in extent and approximately
half of these pages contain illustrations in full colour and
black and white.

They are published jointly by Kestrel Books in hardback
and Puffins in paperback.